Signs of Christ's Return

by
John MacArthur, Jr.

WORD OF GRACE COMMUNICATIONS
P.O. Box 4000
Panorama City, CA 91412

All Scripture quotations, unless noted otherwise, are from the *New Scofield Reference Bible,* King James Version. Copyright © 1967 by Oxford University Press, Inc. Reprinted by permission.

Library of Congress Cataloging in Publication Data

MacArthur, John F.
  Signs of Christ's return.

  (John MacArthur Bible studies)
  1. Eschatology—Biblical teaching.   2. Second
Advent—Biblical teaching.   3. Bible—Criticism,
interpretation, etc.   I. Title.   II. Series:
MacArthur, John F.   Bible studies.
BS2545.E7M22   1987   236'.9   87-5473
ISBN 0-8024-5311-2

1 2 3 4 5 6 7 Printing/LC/Year 91 90 89 88 87

Printed in the United States of America

Contents

These Bible studies are taken from messages delivered by Pastor-Teacher John MacArthur, Jr., at Grace Community Church in Panorama City, California. These messages have been combined into a 7-tape album entitled *Signs of Christ's Return* I (available April 13, 1987) and an 8-tape album entitled *Signs of Christ's Return* II (available August 10, 1987). You may purchase this series either in attractive vinyl cassette albums or as individual cassettes. To purchase these tapes, request the albums *Signs of Christ's Return* I and II, or ask for the tapes by their individual GC numbers. Please consult the current price list; then, send your order, making your check payable to:

WORD OF GRACE COMMUNICATIONS
P.O. Box 4000
Panorama City, CA 91412

Or call the following number:
818-982-7000

1
The Signs of Christ's Coming—Part 1

Outline

Introduction
A. The Bible's Comments on the Future
B. The Jews' Curiosity About the Future
   1. The oppression
   2. The optimism
   3. The outline
   4. The oversight
C. The Disciples' Comprehension of the Future
   1. Their awe at the Lord's prediction
      a) An inconceivable consummation
      b) An immediate confirmation
   2. Their anticipation of the Lord's presence
      a) The statement
      b) The specifics
         (1) About the Lord's coming
         (2) About the end of the age

Introduction

In Matthew 24-25 appears a sermon given by our Lord to the disciples on the Mount of Olives. Appropriately, that sermon is known as the Olivet discourse. Its theme is the second coming of Christ. The Lord talks about His return, the end of the present age, and the establishment of His kingdom.

The sermon in this portion of Scripture was given in response to a question from the disciples. The answer given by Jesus is the longest answer to any question recorded in the New Testament. The insights given in the answer are essential for understanding the future.

A. The Bible's Comments on the Future

The Bible says much about the future. The Old Testament books of Isaiah, Ezekiel, Daniel, and Zechariah and the New Testament book of Revelation all comment extensively on that subject. In fact, people who want to learn more about the coming of the Lord and the end times sometimes overlook Matthew 24-25 in their pursuit to study the other books. Yet Matthew 24-25 presents Christ's own words regarding the end times; therefore it is worthy of our attention.

Unfortunately, Matthew 24-25 is a misunderstood portion of Scripture. There are many different viewpoints and interpretations of what Jesus was saying; you'll learn them as we go through our study. Like many other passages in Scripture, Matthew 24-25 is not as complicated as many people make it out to be. Jesus' teaching is straightforward. It helps to imagine that you know as much as the disciples did when they were listening to Christ. Matthew 24-25 *can* be understood, and it can have a far-reaching impact on our lives.

The Current Interest in Future Events

Everyone is curious about the future. Some people want to know what will happen to the economy so they can make the right investments. There are many reasons for wanting to understand the future, and man has always sought to know the unknown.

The preoccupation with future events is not limited to those who study the Bible. Throughout human history, there have been seers, prophets, prognosticators, witch doctors, fortune-tellers, and religious leaders who try to take a leap into the future and report back to those in the present so that people might have a better understanding of how they should live.

Before we begin studying Matthew 24-25, it's necessary for us to understand the setting of the sermon.

B. The Jews' Curiosity About the Future

The Jewish people of Jesus' day wanted to know what the future held. They were a noble people capable of ruling themselves and forming a meaningful society. However, the Israelites had known oppression for most of their history, and by the time of Jesus, they were anxious for it to cease. The Jewish people longed for the Messiah to come. They knew that when He came, He would make things right and overthrow their oppressors—that He would establish again the kingdom in Israel and fulfill God's promises of peace.

Now we can understand why the Jews were interested in eschatology. The English word *eschatological* is translated from the Greek word *eschatos,* meaning "the last thing." Eschatology is the study of the last days or the end times.

1. The oppression

   Let's consider the oppression the Jewish people experienced from the time Israel split into two separate kingdoms up to the time of Christ. First the Assyrians took the northern ten tribes into captivity. Then the remaining southern tribes were taken into captivity by Babylon. They were successively ruled by the Medes and the Persians, the Greeks, and finally in Christ's time, the Romans. In John 8:33 the Jewish leaders tell Jesus that in spirit they were never in bondage to any man. They were looking forward to the day when they would be ruled by a righteous king and know the blessedness promised to them in the Old Testament.

2. The optimism

   The Jewish people knew that the Old Testament talked of a bright future. They knew they could anticipate a Messiah who would come and reestablish the reign of David on the earth. They longed for the time when Jerusalem would dwell in prosperity and safety forever. So the Jewish people were filled with hope for the future. No doubt they relished God's prophetic promises in the Old Testament. I'm sure they looked forward to the fulfillment of Isaiah 9:6-7, which says, "Unto us a child is born, unto us a son is given, and the government shall be upon his shoulder; and his name shall be called Wonderful, Counselor, The Mighty God, The Everlasting Father, The Prince of Peace. Of the increase of his government there shall be no end, upon the throne of David, and upon his kingdom, to order it, and to establish it with justice and with righteousness from henceforth even forever."

Another prophetic statement the Jewish people exulted in appears in Isaiah 11:1-2: "There shall come forth a rod out of the stem of Jesse, and a Branch shall grow out of his roots; and the Spirit of the Lord shall rest upon him, the spirit of wisdom and understanding, the spirit of counsel and might, the spirit of knowledge and of the fear of the Lord." Jeremiah 23:5 speaks of a future time when the Lord will "raise unto David a righteous Branch, and a King shall reign and prosper, and shall execute justice and righteousness in the earth." Jeremiah 30:9 reiterates that promise. Someday, Israel will become like a flower in full bloom under the blessing of God. Both Zechariah and Daniel spoke of Israel's future. Daniel said there will be a great holocaust someday (Dan. 12:1) but that in the end a great stone (Christ) will smash the kingdoms of the earth to make way for God's eternal kingdom (Dan. 2:44-45).

So by the time Jesus came to earth, the Jewish people were looking forward to the eschatological events the prophets spoke of. They had derived their information from Daniel, Zechariah, Isaiah, Jeremiah, and Ezekiel. Much extrabiblical literature written around the time of Christ shows us what the Jewish people believed about the future. Some examples are the Ethiopic Book of Enoch, the Psalms of Solomon, the Assumption of Moses, the Book of Jubilees, the Ascension of Isaiah, 3 and 4 Esdras, the Apocalypse of Baruch, the Secrets of Enoch, and the Sibylline Oracles.

3. The outline

In Emil Schürer's *A History of the Jewish People in the Time of Jesus Christ* are excerpts from some of the extrabiblical Jewish literature on eschatology ([Edinburgh: T & T

Clark, 1893], pp. 154-87). The following outline is borrowed from it.

a) The expectation of tribulation

The Jewish people believed that before the Messiah came would be a time of terrible tribulation. Just as a woman experiences much pain immediately before she gives birth to a child, so would the nation of Israel suffer before the coming of the kingdom of the Messiah. That viewpoint is biblically supported by Zechariah 14. It is also mentioned in the following passages of extrabiblical literature:

(1) 2 Baruch 27

"And honour shall be turned into shame, and strength humiliated into contempt, and probity destroyed, and beauty shall become ugliness . . . and envy shall rise in those who had not thought aught of themselves, and passion shall seize him that is peaceful, and many shall be stirred up in anger to injure many, and they shall rouse up armies in order to shed blood, and in the end they shall perish together with them."

The Jewish people anticipated a time of moral decay, hatred, and war in the world prior to the coming of the Messiah.

(2) 4 Esdras 9:3

Here we read that there will be quaking of places, tumult of peoples, scheming of nations, confusion of leaders, disquietude of princes.

(3) Sibylline Oracles

"From heaven shall fall fiery swords down to the earth. Lights shall come, bright and great, flashing into the midst of men; and earth, the universal mother, shall shake in these days at the hand of the Eternal. And the fishes of the sea and the beasts of the earth and the countless tribes of fly-

11

ing things and all the souls of men and every sea shall shudder at the presence of the Eternal and there shall be panic. And the towering mountain peaks and the hills of the giants he shall rend, and the murky abyss shall be visible to all. And the high ravines in the lofty mountains shall be full of dead bodies and rocks shall flow with blood and each torrent shall flood the plain. . . . And God shall judge all with war and sword, and there shall be brimstone from heaven, yea stones and rain and hell incessant and grievous. And death shall be upon the four-footed beasts. . . . Yea the land itself shall drink of the blood of the perishing and beasts shall eat their fill of flesh" (3:363ff).

(4) The Mishna

"Arrogance increases, ambition shoots up, that the vine yields fruit yet wine is dear [expensive]. The government turns to heresy. There is no instruction. The synagogue is devoted to lewdness. Galilee is destroyed, Gablan laid waste. The inhabitants of a district go from city to city without finding compassion. The wisdom of the learned is hated, the godly despised, truth is absent. Boys insult old men, old men stand in the presence of children. The son depreciates the father, the daughter rebels against the mother, the daughter-in-law against the mother-in-law. A man's enemies are his house-fellows" (*Sota* ix.15).

The Jews didn't know it, but their theology was premillennial. They anticipated a time of turmoil around the world prior to the coming of Messiah.

b) The announcer like Elijah

The Jewish people believed that during the Tribulation a herald would come announcing the immediate arrival of the Messiah. That herald would be like Elijah. Just as the Messiah is not David—but like David—so the herald would be like Elijah. It is interesting that the Jews were drawn toward John the Baptist when he began his ministry because he was much like Elijah. John the Baptist would have been the forerunner to the Tribulation if the Jews had received Christ and His kingdom. But because they rejected Him, the kingdom was postponed. Therefore there has to be another like Elijah who comes prior to the return of the King. Despite their rejection of Christ, the Jews recognized there would be a herald announcing Messiah's coming. In fact, Jewish oral law stated that any money or property of disputed ownership had to be kept unclaimed until Elijah came, for he would set everything right.

c) The appearing of the Messiah

The Jews said that after the one like Elijah came, the divine King Himself would come to establish His kingdom in glory and vindicate God's people.

d) The war against the Messiah

According to Schürer, the next event the Jews anticipated was the allying of the nations of the world to fight against the Messiah. In the Sibylline Oracles we read, "The kings of the nations shall throw themselves against this land bringing retribution on themselves. They shall seek to ravage the shrine of the mighty God and of the noblest men whensoever they come to the land. In a ring round the city the accursed kings shall place each one his throne with his infidel people by him. And then with a mighty voice God shall speak unto all the undisciplined, empty-handed people and judgment shall come upon them from the mighty God, and all shall perish at the hand of the Eternal" (3:663ff). The nations would gather in Israel to fight against God, yet God would destroy them all.

In 4 Esdras is written, "It shall be that when all the nations hear his [Messiah's] voice, every man shall leave his own land and the warfare they have one against the other, and an innumerable multitude shall be gathered together desiring to fight against him" (13:33-35). There is coming a time when all other wars will be stopped to begin the war against Messiah. The Bible confirms that the nations of the world will gather to fight the Messiah (Rev. 19:19).

e) The destruction of the nations

When all the nations of the earth gather to war against Christ, He will destroy them. Schürer quotes Philo as saying that Christ will "take the field and make war and destroy great and populous nations." In 4 Esdras we read, "He shall reprove them for their ungodliness, rebuke them for their unrighteousness, reproach them to their faces with their treacheries—and when he has rebuked them he shall destroy them" (12:32-33). Enoch 52:7-9 says, "It shall come to pass in those days that none shall be saved, either by gold or by silver, and none shall be able to escape, and there shall be no iron for war, nor shall one clothe oneself with a breastplate. Bronze shall be of no service, and tin shall not be esteemed, and lead shall not be desired. And all things shall be destroyed from the surface of the earth." The Lord will destroy all the hostile nations; He will render their armor useless.

Remember that Schürer is not talking about the premillennial viewpoint that contemporary dispensationalists adhere to; he's talking about what the Jewish people believed at the time of Christ.

f) The renovation of Jerusalem

The Jewish people believed that after the Messiah came, the city of Jerusalem would be purified and renovated. The book of Enoch says of the city, "All the pillars were new and the ornaments larger than those of the first" (90:28-29).

g) The regathering of the Jewish people

Once the city of Jerusalem is renovated, the Jews said there will be a mass influx of Jews to the city. In fact, the Jews have a daily prayer that says, "Lift up a banner to gather our dispersed and assemble us from the four ends of the earth."

In the eleventh psalm of Solomon it is written, "Blow ye in Zion on the trumpet to summon the saints, cause ye to be heard in Jerusalem the voice of him that bringeth good tidings; for God hath had pity on Israel in visiting them. Stand on the height, O Jerusalem, and behold thy children, from the East and the West, gathered together by the Lord; from the North they come in the gladness of their God, from the isles afar off God hath gathered them. High mountains hath he abased into a plain for them; the hills fled at their entrance. The woods gave them shelter as they passed by; every sweet-smelling tree God caused to spring up for them, that Israel might pass by in the visitation of the glory of their God. Put on, O Jerusalem, thy glorious garments; make ready thy holy robe; for God hath spoken good for Israel forever and ever, let the Lord do what he hath spoken concerning Israel and Jerusalem; let the Lord raise up Israel by His glorious name. The mercy of the Lord be upon Israel forever and ever."

The Jewish people correctly understood the Old Testament prophets regarding the end times. Many people think that belief in Christ's return after the Tribulation to set up the millennial kingdom was expressed only by the Christians in the church age. But the Jewish people of Christ's time adhered to the same viewpoint.

h) The significance of Palestine

The Jews believed that after the regathering, Palestine would become the center of the world, and the nations would become subject to it. They said that the people of the nations would come to Jerusalem to worship the King. The Sibylline Oracles say, "All the isles and the cities shall say, How doth the Eternal love those men! For all things work in sympathy with them and help them. . . . Come let us all fall upon the earth and supplicate the eternal King, to His Temple, for He is the sole Potentate" (3:690ff).

i) The new age

> The Jewish people said that when the Messiah reigned, He would usher in a new age of peace, goodness, and glory that would last forever.

Taking into consideration Jewish beliefs regarding the last times, you can understand the perspective they must have had by Christ's time. They had been under tribulation from the Medes and the Persians, the Greeks, and now the Romans. There was also the Maccabean period, when Antiochus Epiphanes of Greece desecrated the Temple. The treatment they received from the Romans made them feel as if they were in the Tribulation period. Then when John the Baptist came, they thought he was the one like Elijah. Next they saw Jesus, who healed people, raised the dead, fed multitudes. Later on He rode into the city of Jerusalem on Passover week, and people threw palm branches and garments before Him, declaring He was the Messiah (Matt. 21:8-9).

What was the first thing that was supposed to happen after Messiah came, according to the Jews? The nations of the earth were to gather against Him, and He would destroy them. So the Jews thought that if Jesus was indeed the Messiah, He would start a war, and naturally the Romans would be the first people attacked. Once the holocaust was over with, He would purify Jerusalem and do away with false religion and hypocrites. Then true worship would take place in the glorious Temple described in Ezekiel 40-48, the Jews would be regathered, and the eternal kingdom would be established. That's what the disciples were thinking.

4. The oversight

You may wonder why the disciples didn't consider the Lord's statement that He would soon die. In John 12:24 He says, "Except a grain of wheat fall into the ground and die, it abideth alone; but if it die, it bringeth forth much fruit." However, the disciples couldn't see how Christ's death fit into the eschatological scenario in their minds. All they could see was coming glory. They didn't understand that the Messiah had to die and that He would return after a long period of time. That time period is known as a mystery because it was not revealed in the Old Testament (Eph. 3:1-9). The Old Testament prophets and Christ's disciples had visualized all the end-time events happening at once after Christ's first coming. The disciples thought everything was right on schedule: the Jewish people were experiencing tribulation, John the Baptist was like Elijah, and the Messiah had come.

Judas probably thought everything was on schedule. That's why he remained a disciple for as long as He did. He never really believed in all that Christ was, but he wanted to remain long enough to play an important role in the coming kingdom. He was motivated by greed. But after the sermon about the end times in Matthew 24-25, the first thing Jesus says in chapter 26 is this: "Ye know that after two days is the feast of the passover, and the Son of man is betrayed to be crucified" (v. 2). Judas's hopes were smashed. He expected the grandeur of the coming kingdom, but Jesus said He was going to die. Thus he decided to betray Christ for whatever money he could get (Matt. 26:14-16).

To see what started the Olivet discourse as recorded in Matthew 24-25, let's look at what is happening at the end of Matthew 23. Jesus had been teaching all day at the Temple on the Wednesday of Passover week. The Jewish religious leaders asked Him some questions, and He answered by condemning them. He pronounced judgment upon them, saying, "Your house is left unto you desolate. For I say unto you, Ye shall not see me henceforth, till ye shall say, Blessed is he that cometh in the name of the Lord" (vv. 38-39). Judgment would soon come upon the nation of Israel, and they would not be redeemed until the nation recognized Him as the Messiah.

When the Lord makes that statement in Matthew 23:38-39, the disciples think it is time for Him to destroy the nations. With that in mind, they ask the Lord a question in Matthew 24:3: "Tell us, when shall these things be? And what shall be the sign of thy coming, and of the end of the age?" Im-

17

plied in the word *when* is the thought that the second coming would be soon—as soon as tomorrow or next week. The disciples thought they had reached the end of the age.

C. The Disciples' Comprehension of the Future

1. Their awe at the Lord's prediction

In Matthew 24:1-2 we read, "Jesus went out, and departed from the temple; and his disciples came to him to show him the buildings of the temple. And Jesus said unto them, See ye not all these things? Verily I say unto you, There shall not be left here one stone upon another, that shall not be thrown down."

Jesus walked out of the Temple with His disciples right after He said, "Your house is left unto you desolate" (Matt. 23:38). Referring to the Temple, He did not call it the Father's house (as in John 2:16). That's because God had already left. It was *Ichabod*, which means "the glory is departed" (1 Sam. 4:21; cf. Ezek. 9:3; 10:4; 11:23). The word *desolate* (Gk., *erēmos*) means "abandoned to ruin."

a) An inconceivable consummation

After Jesus said that one stone wouldn't be left on top of another, the disciples were confused. They couldn't figure out how that could happen. The Temple was massive, and it was more than one building. It was surrounded by a huge wall, and it occupied a large flat area on the top of a mountain. Enclosed within the wall were other buildings that were a part of the Temple area. All that was supported by a retaining wall to the south and the west—a wall that supported the mountain. To the west was a natural slope and to the north a flat area. It was a long distance down from the Temple wall to the bottom of the retaining wall. The top of the Temple's south wall may be where Satan asked Jesus to jump when he tried to tempt the Lord, because it's such a tremendous drop (Matt. 4:5).

The Temple and its surrounding structure were like a fort. No doubt the disciples were in awe of it; they were country men used to little houses on rolling hills. The Temple was so massive that it was inconceivable it could be torn down. Mark 13:2 mentions the greatness of the Temple buildings, and Luke 21:5 says the Temple was adorned with beautiful stones and gifts. First-century Roman historian Tacitus said the Temple was of immense wealth and that it was an excellent fortress (*Histories* V.viii). The Talmud, the codification of Jewish law, states there was no finer building (*Baba Bathra* 4a). It was Herod the Great who had the Temple built. However, Herod was not a Jew, so the Jewish people wondered if the final Temple might be built by someone who was.

The Temple was a formidable place. Some of the stones used in constructing it were forty feet long, twelve feet high, and twelve feet wide. How the builders lifted and carried stones weighing up to one hundred tons is hard to imagine. Some of the large stones had to be lifted two or three hundred feet from the bottom of the south retaining wall to the top of the wall around the Temple. It was a massive undertaking. Some individual stones are as long as eighty-five feet. Thus you can understand the disciples' amazement when Jesus said the Temple would be left desolate. How could such a busy place that was the hub of Jewish life be abandoned to ruin? Even though the Jews expected the Temple to be replaced with the glorious Temple recorded in Ezekiel 40-48, the disciples still couldn't imagine the complete destruction of the Herodian Temple.

b) An immediate confirmation

Jesus knew what the disciples were thinking, so He said, "Verily I say unto you, There shall not be left here one stone upon another, that shall not be thrown down" (Matt. 24:2). The Lord reaffirmed that the Temple would be left desolate. I've stood at the foot of the western wall that was a part of the Herodian Temple, as well as at the cornerstones in the southeast and southwest corners. They've been there since the time of Christ, and they don't look as if anything could move them. They give a small idea of what the Temple must have been like.

If the western wall is still standing, does that contradict Jesus' statement that not one stone would be left on top of another? No, because the western wall and the cornerstones were stones that held up the retaining wall. They weren't a part of the Temple or Temple wall itself; the retaining wall was there to help hold the mountain in place. Therefore, Jesus was correct when He said that not one stone of the Temple would be left on another. First-century Jewish historian Josephus said the city was so leveled that future visitors had no reason to believe the city had ever been inhabited (*Wars* VII.i). The Romans completely tore apart the Temple in A.D. 70. Jesus said, "There shall *not be left* here one stone upon another" (emphasis added). The phrase "not be left" is a double negative in the Greek text. The Temple would be completely destroyed.

Once the Lord spoke of the destruction of the Temple, the disciples probably thought Jerusalem was about to be renovated, and that the Tribulation was over. They were filled with hope.

2. Their anticipation of the Lord's presence

Matthew 24:3 begins by saying that the Lord and the disciples were on the Mount of Olives. That means they would have gone down the back side of the Temple mount, crossed the Kidron Valley over a brook, and gone up to the top of the Mount of Olives. The view from there was breathtaking, and by that time the sun was setting over the white limestone buildings of Jerusalem. Even today you can see the same spectacular view, the major difference being the Dome of the Rock and the Mosque of Omar glistening in the setting sun instead of the massive Temple. The disciples were probably thinking that everything would now come to a great climax in the most glorious moment of Israel's history.

a) The statement

In that setting, the disciples came to Jesus privately, saying, "Tell us, when shall these things be?" (v. 4). They asked Him when the desolation of Jerusalem would take place, referring to what Jesus said previously (Matt. 23:38-39). They didn't know there would be a long period of time between the destruction of Jerusalem and Christ's return in full glory.

The disciples wanted to know what would indicate the coming of the end of the age. Would there be darkness? a brilliant light? an angel from heaven? a trumpet blast? The disciples were excited and anxious. Even after the Lord's resurrection they still expected the kingdom to come right away. In Acts 1:6 they ask Christ, "Lord, wilt thou at this time restore again the kingdom to Israel?" When Christ died the disciples were despondent, but the resurrection heightened their hopes even more than before. When they saw Him out of the grave, they thought the time had come for the kingdom to be set up. Luke 19:11 says that Jesus "spoke a parable, because he was near to Jerusalem, and because they [the Jewish people] thought that the kingdom of God should immediately appear."

b) The specifics

(1) About the Lord's coming

The word *coming* in Matthew 24:3 is translated from the Greek word *parousia*. It means "to be around" or "to be present." The best way to translate the verse might be, "What shall be the sign of Your full presence?" The disciples were referring more to the Lord's permanent presence than to His coming. *Parousia* is also used in verses 27, 37, and 39. Because the Lord used it frequently to refer to His return, the New Testament writers did the same (James 5:8; 2 Pet. 3:4; 1 John 2:28). *Parousia* became synonymous with Christ's arrival to set up His kingdom. However, when the disciples ask about the Lord's coming in

21

Matthew 24:3, they are saying, "When are You going to arrive in Your full messianic revelation? When will You become all that we anticipate You to be?" They didn't think in terms of His leaving and returning; they simply thought the Lord would soon make a transition to setting up His kingdom.

(2) About the end of the age

At the end of Matthew 24:3 the disciples ask the Lord, "What shall be the sign . . . of the end of the age?" The phrase "the end of the age" is translated from the Greek phrase *sunteleias tou aiōnos*. It appears five times in Matthew's gospel. *Sunteleias* means "the complete end." So the disciples were asking, "When is the final end of man's age?"

In Matthew 28:20 Jesus says to the disciples, "Lo, I am with you always, even unto the end of the age." He will be with us until the final end. In the parable of the wheat and the tares, Jesus said, "The harvest is the end of the age; and the reapers are the angels. As, therefore, the tares are gathered and burned in the fire, so shall it be in the end of this age" (Matt. 13:39-40). The phrase is used twice in those verses. The end of the age is when God separates the wheat from the tares and sends the tares to hell. Verses 42-43 say He "shall cast them into a furnace of fire; there shall be wailing and gnashing of teeth. Then shall the righteous shine forth as the sun in the kingdom of their Father." The phrase is used again in Matthew 13:49-50: "So shall it be at the end of the age; the angels shall come forth, and separate the wicked from among the righteous, and shall cast them into the furnace of fire; there shall be wailing and gnashing of teeth." "The end of the age," then, refers to the time when God comes in ultimate, final judgment and sends unbelievers to hell and takes believers into His presence.

What sign were the disciples to look for that would indicate the end of the age? When would they know that ultimate judgment was about to take place? When will that happen? Those questions prompted the Lord's sermon in Matthew 24-25.

The Lord's answer begins in verse 4. He answered the question the disciples asked but said nothing more about the destruction of Jerusalem. That's because He knew the destruction would have nothing to do with His return. The judgment enacted on Israel in A.D. 70 was for the unregenerate, Christ-rejecting Jews of that time. It was only a small taste of the judgment to come at the end of the age when the Messiah returns in full glory. That is the theme of the sermon known as the Olivet discourse. The Lord took His disciples from their moment in history all the way into the far future, when He returns to set up His kingdom in glory.

Focusing on the Facts

1. Why is Matthew 24-25 worthy of our attention (see pp. 7-8)?
2. Why were the Jewish people of Jesus' day especially curious about the future (see p. 9)?
3. What Scripture verses gave the Jewish people optimism about the future (see pp. 9-10)?
4. According to extrabiblical Jewish literature, what did the Jews believe would happen in the coming Tribulation (see pp. 11-12)?
5. What is supposed to happen before Christ comes according to Jewish eschatological beliefs (see p. 12)?
6. What did the Jewish people believe would happen to Jerusalem after the Messiah came? What remaining three things were supposed to happen according to their eschatological viewpoint (see pp. 14-16)?
7. What oversight did the disciples make in their anticipation of the coming kingdom (see pp. 16-17)?

8. When the Lord said, "Your house is left unto you desolate" (Matt. 23:38), what did the disciples think was going to happen (see p. 17)?
9. Why was Christ's declaration regarding the Temple (Matt. 24:2) so hard for the disciples to believe (see pp. 18-19)?
10. What did the disciples ask Jesus after He made that declaration (Matt. 24:2)? Why (see p. 21)?
11. Explain the significance of the phrase "the end of the age" (see p. 22).

Pondering the Principles

1. God keeps His promises. When Christ said, "Repent; for the kingdom of heaven is at hand" (Matt. 4:17), the Jewish people rejected Him. Thus the kingdom God promised to Israel was postponed. God could have eliminated the kingdom altogether because of Israel's rejection, but He didn't do that. According to Zechariah 13:1, there is coming a day when the fountain of salvation will be opened up to the line of Israel, and the nation will be regenerated. Christ's eternal kingdom *will* come; God's promise *will* come true. That applies to all the other promises God made in the Bible. Think of some promises that are especially meaningful to you, and praise God for how He has made or will make them a reality in your life.

2. God's sovereignty is evident in Matthew 24:2. Jesus said the Temple in Jerusalem would be completely destroyed. Just as He said, the Romans completely destroyed it in A.D. 70. God is in full control of everything that happens—even to the point of leading the Romans against Jerusalem. Since God can control major events as that, surely He can control the circumstances in your life. However, you won't always understand the purpose for every situation in your life. The key is trusting in God's sovereignty and His promise that "all things work together for good to them that love God" (Rom. 8:28). In every situation, yield yourself to God, and ask Him to work out His sovereign will, knowing that it will be carried out to His greater glory and your greatest good.

2
The Signs of Christ's Coming—Part 2

Outline

Introduction

Review
A. The Bible's Comments on the Future
B. The Jews' Curiosity About the Future
C. The Disciples' Comprehension of the Future
    1. Their awe at the Lord's prediction
    2. Their anticipation of the Lord's presence

Lesson
    3. Their application of the Lord's prophecy
        a) The Old Testament perspective
        b) The New Testament perspective
D. The Lord's Clarification About the Future
    1. The interpretations pointing to the past
    2. The indicators pointing to the future
        a) The birth pains
            (1) The concept
            (2) The confirmation
        b) The end of the age
        c) The worldwide teaching of the gospel
        d) The abomination of desolation
        e) The incomparable Tribulation
        f) The chaos in the heavens
        g) The parable of the fig tree
I. There Will Be Deception (vv. 4-5)
    A. The Caution About Deception
    B. The Character of Deception
        1. Depicted
        2. Described

Introduction

Jesus came into the world to save it. He came to Israel to be her Redeemer and Messiah. Yet as the apostle John said, "He came unto his own, and his own received him not" (John 1:11). Jesus gave the Olivet discourse (Matt. 24-25) thirty-three years after entering the world—just as He was about to leave it. He began His ministry by offering Himself to the people of Israel, but they later rejected Him. In two more days He would be executed on a cross by the very people He came to save and rule.

Review

The sermon recorded in Matthew 21-23 was the Lord's last public sermon to the people of Israel. He pronounced judgment on the false leaders of Israel and those who followed them. First He spoke in parables of judgment. Then He directly denunciated the Jewish religious leaders who were leading the people astray (Matt. 23). He ended His message of judgment by saying, "Behold, your house is left unto you desolate. For I say unto you, Ye shall not see me henceforth, till ye shall say, Blessed is he that cometh in the name of the Lord" (vv. 38-39). The phrase "he that cometh in the name of the Lord" is a messianic title. The Jewish nation will not see Christ again until they recognize Him as their Messiah and King. First the Lord pronounced judgment, then He spoke of His future return.

A. The Bible's Comments on the Future (see p. 8)

B. The Jews' Curiosity About the Future (see pp. 9-18)

C. The Disciples' Comprehension of the Future

    1. Their awe at the Lord's prediction (see pp. 18-20)

2. Their anticipation of the Lord's presence (see pp. 20-23)

The conclusion of Christ's message no doubt gave the disciples great hope. They were looking forward to the establishment of Christ's kingdom; they had waited for it a long time. They just heard Jesus say He would bring judgment and then come in the name of the Lord. They saw those two events as taking place in close connection with one another, according to their understanding of the Old Testament prophets. The disciples believed they were about to enter the messianic kingdom. Luke 19:11 says that Jesus "spoke a parable, because he was near to Jerusalem, and because they thought that the kingdom of God should immediately appear." From the time Christ approached Jerusalem, the disciples anticipated the kingdom.

Lesson

3. Their application of the Lord's prophecy

The disciples didn't know there would be a long time period between Christ's first and second comings. They had no idea that two thousand or more years would go by before He returned. The Old Testament prophets didn't indicate it would happen that way. That's why the New Testament calls the church age—the era between Christ's two comings—a mystery hidden in times past (Col. 1:26).

a) The Old Testament perspective

In Isaiah 61 we read some words from the Messiah in anticipation of His coming. Verses 1-3 say, "The Spirit of the Lord God is upon me, because the Lord hath anointed me to preach good tidings unto the meek; he hath sent me to bind up the brokenhearted, to proclaim liberty to the captives, and the opening of the prison to those who are bound; to proclaim the acceptable year of the Lord, and the day of vengeance of our God; to comfort all that mourn; to appoint unto those who mourn in Zion, to give unto them beauty for ashes, the oil of joy for mourning, the garment of praise for the spirit of heaviness, that they might be called trees of righteousness, the planting of the Lord, that he might be glorified."

Verses 4-11 continue with that prophecy. Notice that in verse 1 He says He will "proclaim liberty to the captives." Then in verse 2 He says He will "proclaim the acceptable year of the Lord, and the day of vengeance of our God." The preaching of the gospel and the day of vengeance were seen as a unit. Then in verses 3-10 we read about a time of comfort for mourners and healing for the land. Verse 11 concludes, "As the earth bringeth forth her bud, and as the garden causeth the things that are sown in it to spring forth, so the Lord God will cause righteousness and praise to spring forth before all the nations."

Because Isaiah 61:1-11 is one prophecy, the events spoken of were seen as one unit.

b) The New Testament perspective

Luke 4:16-20 says that Jesus "came to Nazareth, where he had been brought up; and, as his custom was, he went into the synagogue on the sabbath day, and stood up to read. And there was delivered unto him the book of the prophet, Isaiah. And when he had opened the book, he found the place where it was written, The Spirit of the Lord is upon me, because he hath anointed me to preach the gospel to the poor; he hath sent me to heal the brokenhearted, to preach deliverance to the captives, and recovering of sight to the blind, to set at liberty them that are bruised, to preach the acceptance of the year of the Lord. And he closed the book."

Notice that Jesus quoted verse 1 and only part of verse 2 from Isaiah 61. He didn't finish verse 2, which talked about "the day of vengeance of our God." Why didn't He include that? Because that aspect of the prophecy is yet future. What the Jewish people interpreted as one prophecy by Isaiah would, according to Jesus, be fulfilled on two separate occasions. That's why He closed the book after He said He would "proclaim the acceptable year of the Lord" (Isa. 61:2a). The second time He will come in judgment. It wasn't until Jesus came that people realized there would be a first and second coming. Even the disciples didn't know there would be a long period of time during which people become saved before Christ returns to establish His earthly kingdom.

D. The Lord's Clarification About the Future

Because the disciples anticipated Christ's immediate earthly rule, they asked, "Tell us, when shall these things be? And what shall be the sign of thy coming, and of the end of the age?" (Matt. 24:3). What made them feel such anticipation? Because Jesus said the Temple would be devastated (Matt. 24:2). As He answered the disciples' questions, He explained that the kingdom was yet future. The events Christ spoke of will immediately precede His second coming.

1. The interpretations pointing to the past

Some commentators say the events in Matthew 24-25 took place before the destruction of Jerusalem in A.D. 70 or sometime during the church age. But several indicators in the Olivet discourse show that Christ was speaking of a time that has not yet come.

2. The indicators pointing to the future

In Matthew 24:4-14 Jesus describes several signs that will precede His second coming. There will be people claiming to be the Christ (v. 5), deception (v. 5), wars and rumors of wars (v. 6), nation rising against nation (v. 7), famine and earthquakes (v. 7), an abundance of false prophets (v. 11), love grown cold (v. 12), and the gospel heard all over the world (v. 14). Some people believe these signs happened in A.D. 70, but careful study makes clear they are still future.

a) The birth pains

(1) The concept

In Matthew 24:8 Jesus says, "All these [signs] are merely the beginning of birth pangs" (NASB). The Lord was referring to the pain a woman experiences when she gives birth to a child.

When do birth pains occur? Not at conception; nor do they come during a pregnancy. Birth pains come just before the birth of a child. They signal the end of the pregnancy. (Doctors monitor the frequency of a woman's contractions so they know when birth is approaching.) Likewise, the signs in Matthew 24:4-14 will occur immediately before His coming, not during the church age.

(2) The confirmation

Paul said this about the coming of the Lord: "Of the times and the seasons, brethren, ye have no need that I write unto you. For yourselves know perfectly that the day of the Lord so cometh as a thief in the night" (1 Thess. 5:1-2). He was saying, "There is no need for me to teach you about eschatology. You know that the day of the Lord will come suddenly and unexpectedly, just as a thief comes in the night."

Verse 3 continues, "When they shall say, Peace and safety, then sudden destruction cometh upon them, as travail upon a woman with child." Paul illustrated the suddenness of the Lord's coming with the birth pains that come at the end of a pregnancy, just as Jesus did.

Birth pains are infrequent at first. Then they become more frequent, with less time between each successive pain until the child is born. That's exactly what will happen in the end times. The birth pains will start far apart. Each subsequent one will occur in less and less time. Finally, right at the time of Christ's coming, there will be an explosion of concurrent, tragic events all across the earth.

b) The end of the age

Matthew 24:13 says, "He that shall endure unto the end, the same shall be saved." What does "the end" refer to? In verse 6 Jesus says, "The end is not yet." And in verse 3 "the end" is used by the disciples in reference to the end of the age. So Jesus was talking about the end of the age. And since He was talking about those who endure the events in Matthew 24— the birth pains—He must have been referring to those who will be alive at the end of the age. Because the disciples and no one since them has experienced all those events, we know the end of the age has not come yet.

c) The worldwide teaching of the gospel

In Matthew 24:14 Christ says, "This gospel of the kingdom shall be preached in all the world for a witness unto all nations; and then shall the end come." Before the end of the age, the gospel will be preached worldwide. Now that couldn't apply to the time before A.D. 70. Even today there are many places in the world where the gospel has not been preached. But there is coming a day when the gospel will be preached all over the world.

How will the gospel be preached to the whole world? Jesus wasn't talking about a slow, gradual process whereby the gospel would eventually reach the whole world. At the end of the age, the gospel will spread throughout the world by some supernatural, instantaneous means. Everyone on the face of the earth will hear it.

d) The abomination of desolation

Matthew 24:15-16 says, "When ye, therefore, shall see the abomination of desolation, spoken of by Daniel the prophet, stand in the holy place (whosoever readeth, let him understand), then let them who are

31

in Judaea flee into the mountains." Jesus was saying that the great Tribulation will take place when the abomination of desolation stands in the holy place.

What is the abomination of desolation? Daniel 9:27 says that the Antichrist "shall cause the sacrifice and the oblation to cease, and for the overspreading of abominations he shall make it desolate." The Antichrist will go into the Temple sometime during the Tribulation and desecrate it. He will commit sacrilege in the place where the Jewish people worship God. He will do that "even until the consummation" (Dan. 9:27). The Antichrist's actions will occur at a time when God will pour out final judgment. Then Christ will come to make an end of sin (Dan. 9:24) and bring everlasting righteousness.

e) The incomparable Tribulation

In Matthew 24:21 we read, "For then shall be great tribulation, such as was not since the beginning of the world to this time, no, nor ever shall be." Before Christ returns, the world will experience great tragedies.

Daniel 12:1 says, "At that time shall Michael stand up, the great prince who standeth for the children of thy people, and there shall be a time of trouble, such as never was since there was a nation even to that same time." The content of Daniel 11 indicates Daniel was referring to the end times. So, at the end of the age will be the worst time of trouble ever in the history of the world.

f) The chaos in the heavens

Jesus says in Matthew 24:29-30, "Immediately after the tribulation of those days shall the sun be darkened, and the moon shall not give its light, and the stars shall fall from heaven, and the powers of the heavens shall be shaken. And then shall appear the sign of the Son of man in heaven." Christ will come immediately after the great Tribulation of verse 21—a time still future.

g) The parable of the fig tree

> Matthew 24:32-34 says, "Now learn a parable of the fig tree: When its branch is yet tender, and putteth forth leaves, ye know that summer is near; so likewise ye, when ye shall see all these things, know that it is near, even at the doors. Verily I say unto you, This generation shall not pass, till all these things be fulfilled." When you see new leaves developing on a fig tree, you know that it will soon bear fruit. Summer is near. The appearance of the leaves is a sign. Likewise, the occurrence of the signs in Matthew 24 indicates that the Lord's return is near. And the generation that is alive when those signs are fulfilled will not pass away until Christ comes. That tells us the signs in verses 4-14 are reserved for those who live in the end times.
>
> It's apparent that the events of Matthew 24-25 are yet future. It's true that some of the things Jesus said will happen in the end times are happening now: we have wars, earthquakes, and famines, but they will happen in proportions far beyond anything we have known. There are even some amazing things happening in the skies, but nothing has happened that compares to what Matthew 24:29 speaks of.

Have the Events in Matthew 24 Happened Already?

Some people insist the signs in Matthew 24 were to take place when the disciples were alive. They point to Christ's usage of the words *ye* and *you* throughout Matthew 24 to support their argument: "*Ye* shall hear of wars and rumors of wars; see that *ye* be not troubled"; "then shall they deliver *you* up to be afflicted, and shall kill *you*; and *ye* shall be hated"; "when *ye*, therefore, shall see the abomination of desolation"; and "pray that *your* flight be not in the winter" (vv. 6, 9, 15, 20, emphasis added).

Whenever God spoke through a prophet about a future event, He spoke directly to the people who lived during the prophet's lifetime. The use of *ye* or *you* doesn't mean that the people who hear the prophecy have to see its fulfillment. The prophecy speaks to those who are alive at the time it is fulfilled, but is also a warning to those alive at its hearing. Some good examples of that appear in these Old Testament passages: Isaiah 33:17-24, 66:10-14 and Zechariah 9:9.

The signs in Matthew 24:4-14 will take place during the great Tribulation, which is still in the future. Let's look now at the signs that will indicate the end of man's age and the beginning of God's eternal, glorious kingdom. Keep in mind that they will be as birth pains (Matt. 24:8). They will start out slowly and speed up as time goes on. That's what appears to happen with the events that take place after each of the seven seals are opened on the scroll in Revelation 5:1–8:1. When the seventh seal is opened, all of a sudden seven trumpets are sounded in succession, each one announcing the outpouring of God's wrath. After that, seven bowls of wrath are poured out on the earth (Rev. 15-16). The seals may be opened over a period of years, the trumpets sounded over a period of perhaps weeks, and the bowls poured out in a matter of hours or days. The birth pains of Christ's coming will get closer and closer to one another near the end of the age.

I. THERE WILL BE DECEPTION (vv. 4-5)

There have always been false teachers who claim to come in the name of Christ yet lead people astray. But the deception in the end times will be especially bad. During that time, the church will be gone—it will have been raptured. The Olivet discourse doesn't talk about the rapture, but there are other passages that indicate the church won't be around during the Tribulation. Without the church's influence, mankind will be left with no restraints. All hell will break loose.

A. The Caution About Deception

In Matthew 24:4 Jesus says, "Take heed [Gk., *blepō*, "keep your eyes open"] that no man deceive you." During the Tribulation, people will be looking for answers to their problems. Matthew 24:12 says that lawlessness will abound. Because the world will be filled with evil, Jesus warns people to beware of deception so they won't be led astray.

Someday this world will fall apart. It will be filled with people without natural affection (2 Tim. 3:3). Social relationships will be disrupted, and economic chaos will prevail. People will indulge in sin constantly. While everything is collapsing, people will be looking for leaders. Many false prophets will come forward claiming to be messiahs and deliverers. They will offer themselves as the solution to the world's problems. In Matthew 24:5 Christ says, "Many shall come in my name, saying, I am Christ; and shall deceive many." Although there are false christs today, there will be many more in the end times. That's why Christ warned people not to be deceived.

Portions of the Olivet discourse appear in Mark 13 and Luke 21. Luke 21:8 says, "Take heed that ye be not deceived; for many shall come in my name, saying, I am Christ; and the time draweth near. Go ye not, therefore, after them." Christ had great concern because, in the end times, people will be crying desperately for leaders to deliver them. They will seek religious leaders because man has a religious bent to his nature.

In Matthew 24:23-24 Jesus says, "If any man shall say unto you, Lo, here is Christ, or there; believe it not. For there shall arise false Christs, and false prophets, and shall show great signs and wonders, insomuch that, if it were possible, they shall deceive the very elect." The false teachers of the end times won't be like those we see now. Empowered by demons, they will be able to do supernatural signs and wonders. Their deeds will captivate the world.

B. The Character of Deception

1. Depicted

The myriad false christs will ultimately culminate in one false christ known as the Antichrist, who will be indwelt by Satan. Daniel called him the little horn (Dan. 8:9), the king of fierce countenance (Dan. 8:23), and the willful king (Dan. 11:36). In Revelation John called him the beast, and Paul called him the man of sin and the son of perdition (2 Thess. 2:3). He will be so convincing and deceptive that Israel will make a covenant with him, believing he is their deliverer (Dan. 9:27). All the nations of the world will be deceived by him and come under his power.

2. Described

   a) Daniel 8

   Scripture has a lot to say about the Antichrist. Daniel 8:23 says, "In the latter time of their kingdom, when the transgressors are come to the full, a king of fierce countenance, and understanding dark sentences, shall stand up." The phrase "when the transgressors are come to the full" explains why God hasn't yet dealt with the evil in our world. He's waiting for sin to run its full course before He eliminates it from existence forever.

   In the day when transgressions come to the full, a king "understanding dark sentences" will stand up. What does that mean? The Antichrist will have communion with Satan and the demons. He will be a medium who can contact evil spirits. Daniel 8:24-25 says, "His power shall be mighty, but not by his own power; and he shall destroy wonderfully, and shall prosper, and continue, and shall destroy the mighty and the holy people. And through his policy also he shall cause deceit to prosper in his hand; and he shall magnify himself in his heart, and by peace shall destroy many." The Antichrist will use peace and negotiations to bring the world under his power.

   b) Revelation 6

   Revelation 6:2 says that when the Tribulation begins, there will come a rider on a white horse. He will conquer, but he will have only a bow and no arrows. That means he will intimidate and conquer the world without resorting to violence. The Antichrist will be a false rider trying to imitate the true rider on the white horse in Revelation 19—the Lord Jesus Christ.

c) Daniel 11

Daniel 11:36 says this about the Antichrist: "The king shall do according to his will; and he shall exalt himself, and magnify himself above every god, and shall speak marvelous things against the God of gods, and shall prosper till the indignation be accomplished; for that which is determined shall be done." The Antichrist will display his power until the wrath of God has run its course and destroyed him. In the time that he rules, he will blaspheme God. He will "honor the god of fortresses; and a god whom his fathers knew not shall he honor with gold, and silver, and with precious stones, and pleasant things" (Dan. 11:38). The Antichrist will raise up new gods; he will be idolatrous.

d) Revelation 13

The apostle John saw the Antichrist as a powerful beast (Rev. 13). According to verses 4-5 people will ask, "Who is like the beast? Who is able to make war with him? And there was given unto him a mouth speaking great things and blasphemies, and power was given unto him to continue forty and two months [three-and-a-half years]." He will be in power during the latter half of the Tribulation—the second half of the seven-year period described in Daniel 9:24-27.

The Antichrist's power will be great. Revelation 13:6-8 says, "He opened his mouth in blasphemy against God, to blaspheme his name, and his tabernacle, and them that dwell in heaven. And it was given unto him to make war with the saints, and to overcome them; and power was given him over all kindreds, and tongues, and nations. And all that dwell upon the earth shall worship him." What deceit! The world will believe he is the savior they've waited so long for. Verse 11 tells us that another beast, a false prophet, will come alongside the Antichrist. Verses 12-14 say, "He exerciseth all the power of the first beast before him, and causeth the earth and them who dwell on it to worship the first beast. . . . And he doeth great wonders, so that he maketh fire come down from heaven on the earth in the sight of men, and deceiveth them that dwell on the earth."

C. The Creator of Deception

Who will be behind all the deception from the Antichrist? Satan himself. Revelation 12:9 calls him "the great dragon . . . that old serpent, called the Devil and Satan, who deceiveth the whole world."

The Prerequisite to the Lord's Coming

In 2 Thessalonians 2 Paul writes, "Now we beseech you, brethren, by the coming of our Lord Jesus Christ, and by our gathering together unto him, that ye be not soon shaken in mind, or be troubled, neither by spirit, nor by word, nor by letter as from us, as that the day of the Lord is present" (vv. 1-2). Apparently someone was telling the Thessalonians that the day of the Lord had arrived and that Christ's coming was imminent. However, Paul told the Thessalonians not to believe that. Why? Verse 3 says, "Let no man deceive you by any means; for that day shall not come, except there come the falling away first, and that man of sin be revealed, the son of perdition." Before the return of the Lord, the Antichrist will be revealed to the world. He will deceive and oppose many, and exalt himself above God. Until that happens, the Lord won't return. Verses 8-10 say, "Then shall that wicked one be revealed . . . even him whose coming is after the working of Satan with all power and signs and lying wonders, and with all deceivableness of unrighteousness in them that perish."

The first sign of the end of man's age is deception. It will be so effective that the whole world will fall for it. No wonder the Lord says to beware.

Focusing on the Facts

1. According to Luke 19:11, the disciples thought the kingdom of God would immediately appear. What were they not aware of (see p. 27)?

2. Why did Jesus quote only verse 1 and part of verse 2 from Isaiah 61 when He taught in a synagogue (Luke 4:16-20; see pp. 28-29)?
3. According to Matthew 24:4-14, what are some of the signs that will precede Christ's coming (see p. 29)?
4. If the signs in Matthew 24 are _____ _____, then they will occur in the times immediately before Christ's _____ (see p. 30).
5. What will happen in regard to gospel preaching at the end times (see p. 31)?
6. What is the abomination of desolation spoken of in Matthew 24:15-16 (Dan. 9:27; see p. 32)?
7. What will happen in the heavens at the end of the Tribulation (Matt. 24:29-30; see p. 32)?
8. What is one argument people use to say that the events of Matthew 24 have already happened? How is that argument refuted (see pp. 33-34)?
9. According to Matthew 24:4-5, what will happen on a massive scale during the end times? Why (see p. 34)?
10. What warning does Christ give in Matthew 24:23-24 (see p. 35)?
11. Describe what the Antichrist will be like, using Scripture references from Daniel and Revelation (see pp. 36-38).
12. What did Paul say must happen before the Lord returns (2 Thess. 2:3; see p. 38)?

Pondering the Principles

1. In Luke 19:11, we see that the disciples believed that Christ's kingdom was about to be established on earth. They didn't realize there would be a long period of time between Christ's first and second comings, the period we are living in right now. Although they may have been disappointed when they discovered that, the disappointment was far outweighed by the certainty that Christ's kingdom *will* come someday. Do you look forward to Christ's return? Meditate on Revelation 21:1–22:5, and specify what you look forward to in the coming kingdom. Keep eternity in mind in everything you do; don't allow present difficulties or circumstances make you lose sight of the great future God has in store for you.

2. Jesus clearly stated that He will return after the signs in Matthew 24:4-15 have taken place. The time indicators He gave show that He was speaking of an era we have not yet entered. Using Matthew 24:4-15, 23-24, and 2 Thessalonians 2:3, what would you say to someone who says that Christ is ruling over the earth right now, as some cults claim?

3
The Signs of Christ's Coming—Part 3

Outline

Introduction

Review
I. There Will Be Deception (vv. 4-5)

Lesson
II. There Will Be Dissension (vv. 6-7*b*)
   A. The Intensity
      1. According to the Old Testament
         a) The prophecy of Daniel
         b) The prophecy of Zechariah
         c) The prophecy of Haggai
      2. According to the New Testament
         a) Revelation 6
         b) Revelation 9
         c) Revelation 13
         d) Revelation 16
   B. The Injunction
III. There Will Be Devastation (vv. 7*c*-8)
   A. The Extent
   B. The Events
      1. Earthquakes
      2. Famine
      3. Pestilences
      4. Fearful sights
      5. Signs from heaven
IV. There Will Be Desecration (v. 9)
   A. Explaining the Desecration
   B. Examining the Desecration

Introduction

In Matthew 24:3, the disciples ask Jesus a few questions that bring about the great sermon in Matthew 24-25: "Tell us, when shall these things be? And what shall be the sign of thy coming, and of the end of the age?" They wanted to know when the Messiah would judge His enemies, purge Jerusalem, gather the Jewish people scattered throughout the earth, and establish His kingdom. The disciples thought Christ's return was only days away, or at most a few weeks away. But the Lord explained that His coming was off in the future. And in Matthew 24:4-14, He details some of the events that will take place when His return is near.

Review

I. THERE WILL BE DECEPTION (vv. 4-5; see pp. 34-38)

In Matthew 24:4-5 Jesus says, "Take heed that no man deceive you. For many shall come in my name, saying, I am Christ; and shall deceive many." There have been false christs in the past, but in the future an abundance of false messiahs will claim they can deliver the world from absolute chaos.

Lesson

II. THERE WILL BE DISSENSION (vv. 6-7b)

Matthew 24:6-7 says, "Ye shall hear of wars and rumors of wars; see that ye be not troubled; for all these things must come to pass, but the end is not yet. For nation shall rise against nation, and kingdom against kingdom." Some nations will be at war while others will have rumors of war. That can include what we call hot wars or cold wars, and they will be all over the globe.

A. The Intensity

Wars have always been going on in one place or another. However, the Lord is saying in Matthew 24:6-7 that at the end will be worldwide warfare on a scale never before known.

Notice the phrase "ye shall hear" in verse 6. It is a future durative in the Greek text and refers to continual hearing. Christ said that someday people will continually hear of wars and rumors of wars. The subject of war will surface constantly.

1. According to the Old Testament

a) The prophecy of Daniel

Daniel 11 confirms that there will be an increase in the intensity and number of wars. The book of Daniel tells of a time when the Tribulation period will precede the Messiah's setting up His kingdom. Daniel said that the Antichrist will rule a great kingdom basically made up of the territory that composed the Roman Empire (Dan. 7:7-8). Some of the countries of Europe will form a Western confederacy, and the Antichrist will rule them. He will be a threat to the whole world. According to Daniel 9:27, Israel will seek protection from her enemies in the Middle East and sign a covenant with him.

Daniel indicates that the European confederacy will be made up of ten nations (Dan. 2:41-42; 7:8, 20, 24-25). Right now ten nations are members of the European Common Market. The confederacy Daniel spoke of could emerge from those nations.

In Daniel 11:40 we read, "At the time of the end shall the king of the south push at him [probably an African coalition]; and the king of the north [the Soviet Union] shall come against [the Antichrist] like a whirlwind, with chariots, and with horsemen, and with many ships; and he shall enter into the countries, and shall overflow and pass through." Those kings and the Antichrist will converge in the Holy Land. Verses 41-43 continue, "[The Antichrist] shall enter also into the glorious land [Israel], and many countries shall be overthrown, but these shall escape out of his hand, even Edom, and Moab, and the chief of the children of Ammon. He shall stretch forth his hand also upon the countries, and the land of Egypt shall not escape. But he shall have power over the treasures of gold and of silver, and over all the precious things of Egypt; and the Libyans and the Ethiopians shall be at his steps."

The Antichrist will defeat Russia and the king of the south. However, verse 44 says, "Tidings out of the east and out of the north shall trouble him." Apparently the Russian forces will regroup, and there will be a great army from the east. Revelation 9:16 says the army from the east will number 200 million people. The army of Red China passed that mark several years ago. When the Antichrist hears that the armies of the east and the north will attack, he will "go forth with great fury to destroy, and utterly to sweep away many. And he shall plant the tabernacles of his palace between the seas in the glorious holy mountain; yet he shall come to his end, and none shall help him" (vv. 44-45). He will put his palace in the middle of Jerusalem on Mount Zion and establish himself as God. But he will come to an end, and no one will help him.

So Daniel prophesied a war of mind-boggling proportions in the end times. All Western Europe will be involved. Scripture doesn't say if the United States will be in the war. Huge armies from the Soviet Union, Africa, and Red China will all converge in Israel for a major holocaust.

b) The prophecy of Zechariah

Zechariah 14 reiterates Daniel's prophecy about the end times. Verses 1-3 say, "Behold, the day of the Lord cometh, and thy spoil shall be divided in the midst of thee. For I will gather all nations against Jerusalem to battle; and the city shall be taken, and the houses rifled, and the women ravished; and half of the city shall go forth into captivity, and the residue of the people shall not be cut off from the city. Then shall the Lord go forth, and fight against those nations, as when he fought in the day of battle." When the Antichrist comes to his end, he will find no one to help him.

c) The prophecy of Haggai

In Haggai 2:22-23 God says, "I will overthrow the throne of kingdoms, and I will destroy the strength of the kingdoms of the nations; and I will overthrow the chariots, and those who ride in them; and the horses and their riders shall come down, every one by the sword of his brother. In that day, saith the Lord of hosts, will I take thee, O Zerubbabel, my servant, the son of Shealtiel, saith the Lord, and will make thee as a signet; for I have chosen thee, saith the Lord of hosts." That speaks of the time when God will send His own army to destroy the armies of the world and set up the One who comes from the loins of Zerubbabel and David—the Messiah.

There will be great dissension at the end. We can see that beginning to take place. It's as if the world is a powder keg ready for someone to light a match. We live in the constant threat of nuclear war. There is constant strife and fighting all across the globe. The stage is being set for the final holocaust.

2. According to the New Testament

a) Revelation 6

This chapter gives us more details about the great warfare that will come during the end times. In verse 1 Christ begins to open a scroll with seven seals. The seven seals are interesting in a symbolic sense because the Romans used to put seven seals on a person's will so that if it were violated, people would know. In giving the scroll to Christ, God is willing the world to Him. As each seal is broken, certain catastrophic events take place.

Verses 1-2 say that when the first seal is opened, the Antichrist will come as a rider on a white horse to deceive many. He will conquer the world, and many will worship him. In verses 3-5 John writes, "When [Christ] had opened the second seal, I heard the second living creature say, Come. And there went out another horse that was red; and power was given to him that sat on it to take peace from the earth, and that they should kill one another; and there was given unto him a great sword. And when he had opened the third seal, I heard the third living creature say, Come. And I beheld and, lo, a black horse; and he that sat on him had a pair of balances in his hand." Verse 6 explains that when the third seal is broken, there will be famine. There won't be enough food in the world as a result of the wars that happen when the second seal is broken.

In verse 7 the fourth seal is opened, and in verse 8 John says, "I looked, and, behold, a pale horse, and his name that sat on him was Death, and Hades followed with him. And power was given unto them over the fourth part of the earth, to kill with sword, and with hunger, and with death, and with the beasts of the earth." One-fourth of the world's population will be massacred. That means more than 1 billion people by today's standards.

b) Revelation 9

After Christ opens the seven seals we read of the seven trumpet judgments. Let's pick it up at the sixth trumpet: "The sixth angel sounded, and I heard a voice from the four horns of the golden altar which is before God, saying to the sixth angel who had the trumpet, Loose the four angels who are bound in the great river, Euphrates. And the four angels were loosed, who were prepared for an hour, and a day, and a month, and a year, to slay the third part of men. And the number of the army of the horsemen were two hundred thousand; and I heard the number of them. . . . By these three was the third part of men killed, by the fire, and by the smoke, and by the brimstone, which issued out of their mouths. For their power is in their mouth, and in their tails; for their tails were like serpents, and had heads, and with them they do hurt. And the rest of the men who were not killed by these plagues yet repented not of the works of their hands, that they should not worship demons, and idols of gold, and silver, and bronze, and stone, and wood, which neither can see, nor hear, nor walk. Neither repented they of their murders, nor of their sorceries, nor of their fornication, nor of their thefts" (vv. 13-16, 18-21). Even after one-fourth of the world's population is wiped out by war and another third is massacred, some people still won't repent.

c) Revelation 13

The demonic forces and Satan himself won't be the only ones waging war during the end times. Verse 7 says this about the Antichrist—the beast: "It was given unto him to make war with the saints, and to overcome them; and power was given him over all kindreds, and tongues, and nations." He is the one who will massacre the armies of the south, north, and east (Dan. 11:40-44). There will be incessant warfare in the end times.

d) Revelation 16

In verse 13 John sees high-ranking demonic spirits come out of the mouths of the dragon and beast and his false prophet. Verse 14 says, "They are the spirits of demons, working miracles that go forth unto the kings of the earth and of the whole world, to gather them to the battle of that great day of God Almighty." Verse 16 says they will be gathered at a place called Armageddon. Demonic forces will try to get all the armies of the world to destroy Jerusalem to keep Christ from coming back. In the midst of that battle, Christ will return and destroy them all (Rev. 19:11-20).

B. The Injunction

Jesus said not to be troubled when you hear of wars and rumors of wars (Matt. 24:6). Why? Because "all these things must come to pass, but the end is not yet" (Matt. 24:6). The increase in wars won't signal that the end is imminent. Sin will still need to run its full course, and other things have to happen before the second coming. So, even when there are wars and rumors of war, the kingdom won't come yet. It won't be time for the destruction of the ungodly, the renovation of Jerusalem, and the purging of the Temple. That will still be in the future. Deception and dissension will worsen on a worldwide scale.

III. THERE WILL BE DEVASTATION (vv. 7c-8)

The third sign or birth pain Christ talked about was devastation. Matthew 24:7 says, "Nation will rise against nation, and kingdom against kingdom, and in various places there will be famines and earthquakes" (NASB*). There will be famines (Gk., *limos*) and earthquakes (Gk., *seismos*). They will occur in staggering proportions all over the earth in the end times. Mark 13:8 says, "There shall be famines and troubles: these are the beginnings of sorrows." Luke 21:11 says, "Great earthquakes shall be in different places, and famines, and pestilences; and fearful sights and great signs shall there be from heaven." (According to the more reliable Greek manuscripts,

*New American Standard Bible.

48

Matthew didn't mention pestilences, but Luke did. Thus some versions of the Bible include pestilences in Matthew 24:7.) So from Matthew, Mark, and Luke we learn that there will be famines, earthquakes, pestilences, fearful sights, and great signs from heaven during the end times.

A. The Extent

Pestilences are diseases and plagues, fearful sights are horrible events, and signs from heaven are changes in the sky. Even though we see those things happening around us now, they will happen on a scale as never before.

The terrible events of the end times will happen "in various places" (Matt. 24:7). They won't happen here and there from time to time; they will come in large doses in many places at the same time. There will be disasters to an extent never before known. The whole world will self-destruct when sin is allowed to run its full course without restraint.

The Lord is restraining sin and its effects in this age. That preserves the earth. But when He removes His restraints in the rapture of the church, the Tribulation will begin. Second Thessalonians 2 confirms that God will restrain the expression of sin until "that wicked one be revealed" (v. 8). After that, the earth won't be able to handle the evil of the people in it and will begin to crumble. Revelation 9 says that during the Tribulation many of Satan's demons will be released from the "bottomless pit." God will allow them to do signs and wonders that will deceive the wicked.

B. The Events

1. Earthquakes

In Revelation 6:12 John says, "I beheld, when he had opened the sixth seal and, lo, there was a great earthquake." Revelation 16 says, "There were voices, and thunders, and lightnings; and there was a great earthquake, such as was not since men were upon the earth, so mighty an earthquake, and so great. . . . Every island fled away, and the mountains were not found" (vv. 18, 20). Revelation 11:13 says, "The same hour was there a great earthquake, and the tenth part of the city [Jerusalem] fell, and in the earthquake were slain of men seven thousand; and the remnant were terrified, and gave glory to the God of heaven." The end times will be characterized by earthquakes.

2. Famine

Revelation 6:6 speaks of what will happen when the third seal is broken during the Tribulation: "I heard a voice in the midst of the four living creatures say, A measure of wheat for a denarius, and three measures of barley for a denarius, and see thou hurt not the oil and the wine." Those who have oil and wine will be the rich, and everyone else will have to eke out a living. A denarius is one day's wage, and a measure of wheat is one-and-a-half pints. During the Tribulation, one day's wages will earn only a small amount of grain. Food will be scarce; famine conditions will reach disastrous proportions. Verse 8 says that one-fourth of the world's population will be killed by the sword and by hunger. Many people will starve to death.

In Revelation 8:7 we read, "The first angel sounded, and there followed hail and fire mixed with blood, and they were cast upon the earth; and the third part of trees was burnt up, and all green grass was burnt up." The destruction of vegetation will make that famine that much worse. Verse 9 adds that when the second angel sounds his trumpet, one-third of the creatures in the ocean will die and one-third of the ships will be destroyed. Those who depend on the sea for their food or transportation of food will be affected. Verses 10-11 indicate that one-third of the rivers and fountains of water in the earth will become bitter, causing many to die. Verse 12 says, "The third part of the sun was smitten, and the third part of the moon, and the third part of the stars." The cycle of day and night will be thrown off. That will harm the growth of what few crops are left.

3. Pestilences

In Revelation 16 we read of the bowls of wrath that are poured out in rapid-fire succession on the earth. Verse 2 says that the first angel "went, and poured out his bowl upon the earth, and there fell a foul and painful sore upon the men who had the mark of the beast, and upon them who worshiped his image." A terrible plague will bring grievous sores upon people. Verse 3 says, "The second angel poured out his bowl upon the sea, and it became like the blood of a dead man; and every living soul died in the sea." When the seventh seal was opened in Revelation 8, only one-third of the sea turned to blood, but in Revelation 16, it all turns to blood. All the rivers and fountains of water will become blood (v. 4). The sun will scorch people (v. 8), and then the world will be filled with darkness, and everyone will gnaw his tongue in agony (v. 10). There will be many terrible plagues in the end times.

4. Fearful sights

According to Revelation 9, a bottomless pit will open up and many demonic beings will come from it. Men will be tormented by those demons, whose sting will be like that of a scorpion (v. 5). Their torment will be so bad that men will seek death but won't find it (v. 6). The Hebrew name for the leader of those demons is *Abaddon* (v. 11), and his Greek name is *Apollyon*, which means "destroyer"—Satan himself. What a terrifying experience! Verse 15 speaks of a horrible massacre that will take place. Revelation 12:12 says, "Woe to the inhabiters of the earth and of the sea! For the devil is come down unto you." Not only will many demons roam the earth; but also Satan himself. He will bring forth all the evil that his mind can conceive.

Revelation 14:20 speaks of another fearful sight. The bloodshed at Armageddon will be so bad that blood will flow at the height of a horse's bridle for two hundred miles. From the northernmost tip of Israel to the southernmost tip will be one big bloodbath. As we read earlier, Revelation 16 mentions that the sea and fresh water will turn to blood, the sun will scorch people, darkness will come, and people will gnaw their tongues out of pain. Verse 18 says, "There were voices, and thunders, and lightnings." Revelation 18:8 says, "Therefore shall her plagues come in one day, death, and mourning, and famine, and she [the worldwide economic system known as Babylon] shall be utterly burned with fire; for strong is the Lord God who judgeth her." The rest of chapter 18 describes the devastation of Babylon.

5. Signs from heaven

The heavens will fall apart during the Tribulation. Revelation 6:12-13 says, "The sun became black as sackcloth of hair, and the moon became like blood; and the stars of heaven fell unto the earth, even as a fig tree casteth her untimely figs, when she is shaken of a mighty wind." Joel had prophesied that (Joel 2:10), and Peter repeated it in his sermon on the Day of Pentecost (Acts 2:19-20). Just as a mighty wind will shake the figs out of a fig tree, so God will shake the heavens and cause the stars to fall. Verse 14 continues, "The heaven departed as a scroll when it is rolled together; and every mountain and island were moved out of their places." What a horrifying time to be alive.

Revelation 8 also speaks of what will happen in the heavens: "The fourth angel sounded, and the third part of the sun was smitten, and the third part of the moon, and the third part of the stars, so that the third part of them was darkened, and the day shone not for a third part of it, and the night likewise" (v. 12). The calendar, the seasons, and the tides will be thrown off as God's judgment is poured out on the earth. When the final bowl of wrath is poured out, the islands will flee, the mountains won't be found, and hailstones weighing about one hundred pounds will fall from heaven (Rev. 16:20-21).

IV. THERE WILL BE DESECRATION (v. 9)

A. Explaining the Desecration

In Matthew 24:9 Christ says, "Then shall they deliver you up to be afflicted, and shall kill you; and ye shall be hated of all nations for my name's sake." There will be desecration. To desecrate something is to treat a holy thing in an unholy way. The holy people of God will be treated in an unholy way. There will be widespread persecution of the redeemed that will exceed all other persecutions.

The phrase "deliver you up" is a technical term often meaning "to arrest" (cf. Matt. 4:12). During the Tribulation, true believers will be arrested, afflicted, and murdered because they identify with the Lord Jesus Christ. In a passage parallel to the Olivet discourse, Jesus says, "Take heed to yourselves; for they shall deliver you up to councils; and in the synagogues ye shall be beaten" (Mark 13:9). At least in the beginning of the end, Jewish people will persecute those who are believers.

How is it possible for believers to be persecuted during the end times if they are raptured before the Tribulation begins? After the church is raptured, God will send two prophets to proclaim the truth (Rev. 11). They will be murdered (v. 7), but they will rise from the dead (v. 11). Their resurrection will win some people over to Christ. It is those people who will be the objects of persecution from the Jews and the world. They will be delivered up to synagogues. That isn't a remote possibility, because there are many synagogues in Israel now. So believers will be persecuted by Jews and Gentiles. But at the end, God will purge out those rebels from the land (Ezek. 20:38).

B. Examining the Desecration

   1. Why it will happen

      The world will treat God's holy people shamefully. There will be no place to hide because believers will be hated by all the nations. Why will the world hate Christians? Because Jesus said the persecution will be "for my name's sake" (Matt. 24:9). The world hates Christ—it has in the past and will in the future. Its mad hatred will reach its peak when the Antichrist sets up himself against the Lord. Believers have been martyred throughout the history of the church, but it will get worse in the end times.

2. What specifically will happen

Revelation 6:9 says, "When [Christ] had opened the fifth seal, I saw under the altar the souls of them that were slain for the word of God, and for the testimony which they held." The altar represents a place of atonement, so the people under it were saved. From the context we learn they had been massacred during the Tribulation. Verses 10-11 say, "They cried with a loud voice, saying, How long, O Lord, holy and true, dost thou not judge and avenge our blood on them that dwell on the earth? And white robes were given unto every one of them; and it was said unto them that they should rest yet for a little season, until their fellow servants also and their brethren, that should be killed as they were, should be fulfilled." The Lord responded that their blood wouldn't be avenged until all the other saints that were to die during the Tribulation were killed.

Revelation 7:9-10 says, "Lo, a great multitude, which no man could number, of all nations, and kindreds, and peoples, and tongues, stood before the throne, and before the Lamb, clothed with white robes, and palms in their hands, and cried with a loud voice, saying, Salvation to our God who sitteth upon the throne, and unto the Lamb." Who are those people? Verse 14 says, "These are they who came out of the great tribulation, and have washed their robes, and made them white in the blood of the lamb." How did they get out of the Tribulation? They were probably martyred for the sake of the Savior.

In Revelation 9, starting from verse 13, we read of an Eastern army that massacres people all over the world. No doubt that will include many believers. Verse 21 says, "Neither repented they of their murders." In Revelation 11, the two witnesses God sends to testify of Him are murdered. Chapter 12 says that the dragon—Satan—will make war with the remnant (most likely Jewish believers). Revelation 13:7 says he will make war with the saints and overcome them. Revelation 17 says that the great harlot, the false religious system of the Tribulation, will be "drunk with the blood of the saints, and with the blood of the martyrs of Jesus" (v. 6). There will be those who hate believers and "shed the blood of saints and prophets" (Rev. 16:6).

V. THERE WILL BE DEFECTION (vv. 10-13)

A. Because of Persecution

1. They will break away from Christ

   Matthew 24:10 says, "Then shall many be offended, and shall betray one another, and shall hate one another." When Christians start being massacred, anyone who is superficially connected with Christ will reject Him. They will be like the seed that falls in the stony ground—it never develops any depth, and therefore can't take the heat, but it looks good at first (Matt. 13:5-6). When they see the price they have to pay for identifying with Christ, they will become offended and reject Christ. They will also tell the persecutors where they can find true believers to kill them.

Will True Christians Reject Christ During the Tribulation?

Are the defectors Christ talks about in Matthew 24:10 true believers? No. If they had been, they would have continued in the truth. First John 2:19 says anyone who professes to be a Christian but later rejects Christ was never a Christian in the first place. Jesus says in John 8:31, "If ye continue in my word, then are ye my disciples indeed."

Our Lord says this about discipleship in Matthew 10:24-25: "The disciple is not above his teacher, nor the servant above his lord. It is enough for the disciple that he be like his teacher, and the servant like his lord. If they have called the master of the house Beelzebub, how much more shall they call them of his household? Fear them not, therefore; for there is nothing covered that shall not be revealed." Jesus was saying that because people had accused Him of being of Satan, the same thing and more would happen to His disciples. However it's enough for Christians to be like Christ. The true disciple is willing to suffer as the Master suffered.

In Matthew 10 the Lord concludes, "Whosoever, therefore, shall confess me before men, him will I confess also before my Father, who is in heaven. . . . And he that taketh not his cross and followeth after me, is not worthy of me" (vv. 32, 38). The person who isn't willing to suffer or die for Christ—who leaves Christ when persecution comes his way—isn't worthy of being a disciple. A person who belongs to Christ will stay with Him. He is willing to pay the price not because of some special characteristic he has, but because every true believer is given sustaining grace by the Holy Spirit.

Hebrews 3:12 says, "Take heed, brethren, lest there be in any of you an evil heart of unbelief, in departing from the living God." When someone departs from God, he manifests an evil heart of unbelief. Paul told Timothy, "If we deny him, he also will deny us" (2 Tim. 2:12). There are people who outwardly attach themselves to Christianity but leave when things get bad. They get out because they're not willing to pay the price. Luke 9:57-62 tells of people who said they were willing to follow the Lord once they were finished with other things they wanted to do. But Jesus said, "No man, having put his hand to the plough, and looking back, is fit for the kingdom of God" (v. 62).

2. They will betray Christians

Jesus says in Matthew 24:10 that not only will there be defectors, but that those defectors will betray true believers. That's tragic. Mark 13:12 says, "Brother shall betray brother to death, and the father, his son; and children shall rise up against their parents, and shall cause them to be put to death." Even family members will betray one another. Luke 21:16 says, "Ye shall be betrayed both by parents, and brethren, and kinsfolk, and friends; and some of you shall they cause to be put to death."

B. Because of Deception

Some people will defect because they don't want to pay the price of following Christ. Matthew 24:11 says there will be other people who defect because they are deceived: "Many false prophets shall rise, and shall deceive many." In the end times, many false prophets and teachers will arise (cf. Matt. 24:24). They will teach satanic error.

Satan will be running loose in the world during the Tribulation, and he can disguise himself as an angel of light (2 Cor. 11:14). Therefore overt evil will mark the end times, as well as a proliferation of false religions. According to Revelation 17, there will be a wretched worldwide religious system known as the harlot. While the church is Christ's bride, this system will be the prostitute of religion. All kinds of religious deception will flourish as Satan does everything he can to keep people away from Christ. Cults will blossom and deceive those who are superficially interested in Christ. According to Revelation 9:21 people will refuse to repent of their "sorceries." The Greek word translated "sorceries" is *pharmakeia*, which means "drugs." Drugs will probably have a role in the religious deception of the future.

C. Because of Love for Sin

The third element of the future deception is stated in Matthew 24:12: "Because iniquity shall abound, the love of many shall grow cold." Some will defect because they're not willing to pay the price, some because they're deceived, and some because they choose iniquity. The Greek word translated "iniquity" means "lawlessness." People will chose to violate God's law. Sin will abound to the point where it will draw people who are moving toward the truth right back out of it. That's happening even now. There was a girl in the youth department at Grace Church who left when she was enticed by sin. And the wickedness that will engulf the world during the Tribulation will be much more powerful than what we see today. What is only in a gross pornographic magazine today will probably be going on publicly at that time. Such wickedness will cause the love of many to grow cold.

Paul described that wickedness this way: "Men shall be lovers of their own selves, covetous, boasters, proud, blasphemers, disobedient to parents, unthankful, unholy, without natural affection, trucebreakers, false accusers, incontinent, fierce, despisers of those that are good, traitors, heady, high-minded, lovers of pleasures more than lovers of God" (2 Tim. 3:2-4). Lawlessness will run rampant all over the globe. And we are approaching that state rapidly. Whatever interest people might have in Christ will grow cold. Their love of evil will call them away from Him.

Matthew 24:13 says, "He that shall endure unto the end, the same shall be saved." How will you be able to tell who the true believers are? They won't defect from Christ, false teachers won't deceive them, and they won't love evil. Those who endure until the end are the true Christians. They will be delivered from the wrath to come—God's judgment at the end of the age (1 Thess. 1:10). Endurance is always the mark of the saved.

Jesus says in Matthew 10:22, "Ye shall be hated of all men for my name's sake, but he that endureth to the end shall be saved." Jesus was saying that true Christians will go to the end of their lives and endure all that comes their way, thereby demonstrating that they are truly saved. They will be delivered out of this life into the glories of heaven. They are, as Revelation 2:10-11 says, overcomers. They will remain with Christ no matter what the price. Luke 21:19 says, "In your patience possess ye your souls." The faith that perseveres is the faith of the redeemed.

In Revelation 7 we see in white garments those who endured through the Great Tribulation. We also see them in Revelation 19 returning with Christ. They were faithful to Christ in the midst of persecution.

VI. THERE WILL BE DECLARATION (v. 14)

A. The Message

The final birth pain that will signal the imminence of Christ's coming is spoken of in Matthew 24:14: "This gospel of the kingdom shall be preached in all the world for a witness unto all nations; and then shall the end come." In spite of the persecution, defectors, false prophets, demons, iniquity, the Antichrist, wars, earthquakes, famines, and signs in the heavens, there will be a worldwide proclamation of the gospel. Then the kingdom of Christ will come.

B. The Method

How will the gospel be preached throughout the world during the Tribulation? The apostle John says in Revelation 14:6 (just before the bowls of wrath are poured out), "I saw another angel fly in the midst of heaven, having the everlasting gospel to preach unto them that dwell on the earth, and to every nation, and kindred, and tongue, and people." This worldwide preaching of the gospel hasn't happened yet; in Matthew 24:14 Jesus is talking about a future time when an angel will supernaturally proclaim the gospel all around the world before God pours out His judgment at the end of the Tribulation. He will say with a loud voice, "Fear God, and give glory to him; for the hour of his judgment is come; and worship him that made heaven, and earth, and the sea, and the fountains of waters. And there followed another angel, saying, Babylon is fallen, is fallen" (Rev. 14:7-8). Basically they will be saying, "Man's day is over. You had better get right with God." The angels will preach that God judges sin and rewards righteousness. They will call the world to the Savior. After that, the end will come.

Focusing on the Facts

1. What will be different about the wars during the end times (see p. 43)?
2. Who will be involved in the wars prophesied in Daniel 11 (see pp. 43-45)?
3. What are some of the things that will happen when Christ breaks the seals on the scroll in Revelation 6 (see p. 46)?
4. What will the demonic forces of the world do at the end of the Tribulation according to Revelation 16 (see p. 48)?
5. How did Christ say people are to respond when they hear of "wars and rumors of wars" (Matt. 24:6; see p. 48)?
6. What will be the extent of the devastation during the end times (see p. 49)?
7. What will contribute to the famine in the Tribulation (see p. 50)?
8. Describe the pestilences mentioned in Revelation 16 (see pp. 50-51).

9. What does Revelation 6:12-13 say will happen in the heavens during the Tribulation (see p. 52)?
10. What will happen to Christians during the Tribulation? (see pp. 52-53)?
11. If all the Christians on the earth are going to be raptured at the beginning of the Tribulation, where will the Christians who endure the Tribulation come from (see p. 53)?
12. Why will God's people be hated by all the nations in the end times (Matt. 24:9; see p. 53)?
13. During the Tribulation, what will happen to those who are superficially attached to Christ (Matt. 24:10; see p. 55)?
14. Will true Christians reject Christ during the Tribulation? Explain (see pp. 55-56).
15. According to Matthew 24:11, what is one factor that will cause some people to reject Christ (see pp. 56-57)?
16. What is one other element that will cause people superficially attached to Christ to stray away from Him (Matt. 24:12; see p. 57)?
17. What did Jesus mean when He said, "He that shall endure unto the end, the same shall be saved" (Matt. 24:13; see p. 58)?
18. What will be proclaimed worldwide before the coming of Christ, and how will it be proclaimed (see pp. 58-59)?

Pondering the Principles

1. Since the turn of this century, there have been two world wars. Periodically news of devastating earthquakes and famines stretch across newspaper headlines. Tragic things happen daily. Certainly this world is falling apart, but what is happening now pales in comparison to what will happen during the Tribulation. Some Christians fear the prospect of having to live through the Tribulation, but that's an unnecessary fear. First Thessalonians 1:10 and Revelation 3:10 tell us that God will protect His church from the outpouring of His wrath by removing it from the earth. Memorize those verses as a reminder of God's love for His church.

2. Revelation 6:9-11 and 7:9-14 speak of great multitudes who will receive Christ as their Savior during the Tribulation. Evidently the tragic events around them will stir them to acknowledge God as Lord. That is an example to us of how God can use difficult circumstances to call our attention to Him. Read James 1:2-4.

What does it say about how you can benefit from trials? Although you won't always understand your circumstances, you can take comfort in knowing that God will use them to perfect you.

4
The Abomination of Desolation

Outline

Introduction
  A. Isaiah on the Tribulation
  B. Jeremiah on the Tribulation
  C. Daniel on the Tribulation
  D. Zechariah on the Tribulation

Review

Lesson
  I. The Perpetrator of the Abomination
      A. His Empire
      B. His Alliance
      C. His Battles
 II. The Particulars of the Abomination
      A. The Abomination Defined
      B. The Holy Place Identified
III. The Preview of the Abomination
      A. The Forerunner of the Antichrist
      B. The Foretaste of the Abomination
 IV. The Prediction of the Abomination
      A. Daniel 9
          1. The period
          2. The prince
          3. The pollution
      B. Daniel 12
          1. The 1290 days
          2. The 1335 days
  V. The Portrayal of the Abomination

Conclusion

Introduction

People in our world are always wishing for a better day, for a time when the problems that plague human society will be alleviated. However, the message of Scripture is that before there is a better time, there is going to be an infinitely worse time. Our Lord describes that time in Matthew 24:21: "Then shall be great tribulation, such as was not since the beginning of the world to this time, no, nor ever shall be."

Our Lord was not the first to speak of this coming time of trouble (known as the Tribulation). It will involve the whole world but will be especially significant for Israel.

A. Isaiah on the Tribulation

In chapter 10 Isaiah looks forward to the day of the Lord. That will be a time of great judgment, a time when the kingdom of the Messiah will be established and Israel will be saved. Man's work on earth will be complete, and God will rule. Isaiah says in verses 20-23, "It shall come to pass in that day, that the remnant of Israel, and such as have escaped of the house of Jacob, shall no more again lean upon him who smote them, but shall lean upon the Lord, the Holy One of Israel, in truth. The remnant shall return, even the remnant of Jacob, unto the mighty God. For though thy people, Israel, be like the sand of the sea, yet a remnant of them shall return; the full end decreed shall overflow with righteousness. For the Lord God of hosts shall make a full end."

There is coming a time of great stress for Israel, yet a remnant will escape and learn never again to rely on anyone other than the Lord. However, before their salvation, the people of Israel will lean on someone who offers himself for support but then afflicts them.

B. Jeremiah on the Tribulation

Jeremiah 30:5-6 says, "Thus saith the Lord, We have heard a voice of trembling, of fear, and not of peace. Ask now, and see whether a man doth travail with child? Why do I see every man with his hands on his loins, like a woman in

travail [birth pain], and all faces are turned into paleness?"
When Jeremiah looked into the distant future, he didn't
see peace: he saw trembling and fear. The most excruciat-
ing human pain, that of giving birth to a child without an
anesthetic (as women did in that time), symbolizes the
pain of society in the future. Jeremiah saw the world and
Israel in particular in great pain.

Jeremiah goes on to say in verses 7-9, "Alas! for that day is
great, so that none is like it; it is even the time of Jacob's
trouble, but he shall be saved out of it. For it shall come to
pass in that day, saith the Lord of hosts, that I will break
his yoke from off thy neck, and will burst thy bonds, and
strangers shall no more enslave them, but they shall serve
the Lord, their God, and David [the Messiah, David's des-
cendant], their king, whom I will raise up unto them." Jeremiah described a day like no other day—a day of great
judgment and distress, the time of Jacob's trouble. Out of it
is going to come salvation and the raising up of the Messiah and His kingdom.

C. Daniel on the Tribulation

In Daniel 12:1 we read, "At that time shall Michael stand
up, the great prince who standeth for the children of thy
people [the angelic protector of Israel], and there shall be a
time of trouble, such as never was since there was a nation
even to that same time; and at that time thy people shall be
delivered, every one that shall be found written in the
book."

D. Zechariah on the Tribulation

Zechariah 13:8–14:2 says, "It shall come to pass that in all
the land, saith the Lord, two parts in it shall be cut off and
die; but the third shall be left in it. And I will bring the third
part through the fire, and will refine them as silver is refined, and will test them as gold is tested; they shall call on
my name, and I will hear them. I will say, It is my people;
and they shall say, The Lord is my God. Behold, the day of
the Lord cometh, and thy spoil shall be divided in the
midst of thee. For I will gather all nations against Jerusalem
to battle; and the city shall be taken, and the houses rifled,
and the women ravished; and half of the city shall go forth

into captivity, and the residue of the people shall not be cut off from the city." Two out of three in the land of Israel will die. The third will come to the awareness that the Lord is God.

That is a prophetic picture of the time just before the second coming of Christ. It is described in the Olivet discourse by our Lord and in the Old Testament by the prophets. A time of great distress will be followed by the purging and salvation of Israel and the coming of Messiah to establish His glorious eternal kingdom. It should be noted that the rapture of the church is not mentioned in Matthew 24 or 25. The nation of Israel, not the church, is in view here. The rapture of the church is discussed later in the epistles.

Review

Our Lord had just described the general conditions that will be in effect at the time of His return. However, He knew that was not what the disciples were asking because in Matthew 24:3 they ask, "What shall be *the sign* of thy coming, and of the end of the age?" (emphasis added). In verse 15, Jesus describes for the disciples the event that will cause the birth pains of verses 4-14 to begin: "When ye, therefore, shall see the abomination of desolation, spoken of by Daniel the prophet, stand in the holy place."

Lesson

I. THE PERPETRATOR OF THE ABOMINATION

In Daniel 11 we meet the man who will commit the abomination of desolation: the Antichrist. He is referred to here as the willful king. Daniel portrays him as one who does his own will and who doesn't have a natural desire for women. He will have a perverse worship of military power and will magnify himself above all. The Antichrist will flaunt his hatred of the true God and Jesus Christ and attempt to set up his own kingdom in his own power.

A. His Empire

According to Daniel 2:40-43, there will be a revival of the Roman Empire, encompassing much of the territory of the old Roman Empire. Out of the revived Roman Empire will rise a great leader who will hold power in Western Europe.

B. His Alliance

The Antichrist will make an alliance with Israel against the Soviet-Arab alliance (described in Ezek. 38) that will come against them. He is the one spoken of in Isaiah 10: Israel will lean on him, yet he will smite them. In spite of his alliance with Israel, he will turn on them.

C. His Battles

Following the Antichrist's alliance with Israel, armies from the north, south, and east will fight the Antichrist and his Western confederacy, but he will defeat them (Dan. 11:40-45). At this point, after becoming Israel's protector and defeating the world powers, he will commit the abomination of desolation.

II. THE PARTICULARS OF THE ABOMINATION

A. The Abomination Defined

Abomination (Gk., *bdelugma*) refers to that which is abhorrent, detestable, and utterly repulsive to God. It is used in Revelation 17:4-5 of the false religious system known as Mystery Babylon, the harlot. It is used in Revelation 21:27, which says there will be nothing in heaven that is repulsive to God. In the Old Testament, the concept of abomination is predominantly associated with heathen idols—false gods that are detestable to the one true God. The abomination of desolation will be an idolatrous act that will defile the Holy Place.

B. The Holy Place Identified

The "holy place" (Matt. 24:15) has been variously interpreted as the land of Israel, the people of Israel, or the city of Jerusalem. Nonetheless Acts 21:28 tells us quite clearly what it is. Paul had come back to Jerusalem after his third missionary journey. He wanted to reassure the Jews that he was not a traitor to his people. To do this, he went into the Temple to go through a purification ritual with some Jewish men. While Paul was in the Temple, Jews from Asia who knew Paul was a preacher of the gospel found him and started a riot. This was their accusation against Paul: "Men of Israel, help! This is the man that teacheth all men everywhere against the people, and the law, and this place; and further brought Greeks also into the temple, and hath polluted this holy place" (Acts 21:28). The phrase "holy place" in this verse can only be a reference to the Temple. And I don't see any reason for it to mean anything other than that in Matthew 24:15. The Old Testament also refers to the Temple as the Holy Place (cf. Ps. 24:3).

III. THE PREVIEW OF THE ABOMINATION

Matthew 24:15 gives us the key to identifying the abomination of desolation. It is not just any event but the one spoken of by Daniel the prophet, who gives us a preview of it in chapter 11. In describing the sacrilege committed by Antiochus Epiphanes in the second century B.C., Daniel gives us a foretaste of the abomination of desolation that will be committed in the end time by the Antichrist.

A. The Forerunner of the Antichrist

Daniel 11:31 introduces us to an interesting historical figure, who almost all scholars agree is Antiochus Epiphanes. He was a Syrian king who reigned in Palestine from about 175 to 163 B.C. He called himself Epiphanes, which means "the great one." The people called him Epimanes, which means "maniac." Verse 31 says this about him: "Forces shall stand on his part, and they shall pollute the sanctuary of strength, and shall take away the daily sacrifice, and they shall place the abomination that maketh desolate." In that historical act of Antiochus Epiphanes, we have a picture of what the Antichrist will do in the end times.

B. The Foretaste of the Abomination

Antiochus Epiphanes was a great persecutor of the Jewish people. The apocryphal books of 1 and 2 Maccabees describe how he tried to stamp out Jewish religion and in so doing slaughtered thousands of Jewish men, women, and children. In one of the worst acts in Jewish history, Antiochus desecrated the Temple by slaughtering a pig on the altar, forcing the priests to eat pork, and setting up an idol to Zeus. The Jews then abandoned the Temple, not wishing to go into a defiled place. That put a halt to the daily sacrifices (as predicted by Dan. 11:31) until the Jews regained control of the Temple during the Maccabean revolution.

IV. THE PREDICTION OF THE ABOMINATION

Daniel gives a preview of the abomination of desolation in chapter 11, where he describes the career of Antiochus Epiphanes. He gives us a direct prediction of it in two other places.

A. Daniel 9

1. The period

In verse 24 Daniel says, "Seventy weeks are determined upon thy people and upon thy holy city, to finish the transgression, and to make an end of sins, and to make reconciliation for iniquity, and to bring in everlasting righteousness, and to seal up the vision and prophecy, and to anoint the most Holy." The weeks here are weeks of years. Daniel is saying there will be seventy times seven, or 490 years, to the kingdom of the Messiah. Verse 25 tells us when that 490-year period began: "Understand that from the going forth of the commandment to restore and to build Jerusalem." In 445 B.C., King Artaxerxes of Persia issued a decree permitting the Jews to rebuild Jerusalem. From that date, sixty-nine weeks (483 years) were to elapse before the coming of Messiah the Prince (Dan. 9:25). Calculations by Sir Robert Anderson (*The Coming Prince* [Grand Rapids: Kregel, 1954]) and by Harold Hoehner (*Chronological Aspects of the Life of Christ* [Grand Rapids: Zondervan, 1977]) have shown that the period from Artaxerxes' decree to Christ's presentation of Himself as Israel's Messiah (at His triumphal entry into Jerusalem) is 483 years—to the very day.

That leaves one week unaccounted for. We know that the first sixty-nine weeks ended when Messiah came, but the seventieth week hasn't come yet. That leaves us with an undetermined time gap between the sixty-ninth and the seventieth weeks.

2. The prince

Daniel introduces us to a second prince in verse 26. This is not a reference to Antiochus Epiphanes because this prince is connected with the second coming of the Messiah, which is still future. He will cause desolation to come upon Israel. Verse 27 says he will make a covenant with Israel for one week (seven years). In the middle of that week (the seventieth week) he will cause the sacrifice and the offerings to cease, just as Antiochus Epiphanes did.

3. The pollution

Halfway through the seventieth week (after three-and-a-half years), the prince will cause the sacrifice to stop, and then he will bring "the overspreading of abominations" (v. 27). That is a reference to the abomination of desolation. He will do this "until the consummation, and that determined shall be poured upon the desolate"—until the end of the Tribulation.

B. Daniel 12

1. The 1290 days

In verse 11 Daniel once again predicts the abomination of desolation: "From the time that the daily sacrifice shall be taken away, and the abomination that maketh desolate set up, there shall be a thousand two hundred and ninety days." According to Revelation 12:6, there will be 1260 days from the middle of the seventieth week until the end, but Daniel mentions here 1290 days. I think the best explanation of the apparent discrepancy is that the extra thirty days Daniel mentions take place after the Tribulation has ended, giving us the time frame in which the sheep-and-goat judgment (Matt. 25:31-46) takes place. At that time, all the people still on the earth will be gathered together before the Lord to be judged.

2. The 1335 days

Verse 12 reads, "Blessed is he that waiteth, and cometh to the thousand three hundred and five and thirty days." That verse speaks of forty-five more days that will follow the sheep-and-goat judgment. I believe that will be a transition time for the setting up of the kingdom. The Lord will establish His throne in Jerusalem, place believers as His envoys throughout the world, and start disseminating the rules and principles for the millennial kingdom.

Prophecy is specific: the last three-and-a-half years of the Tribulation, during which all the horrors of the Tribulation time are concentrated, will begin with the abomination of desolation—the desecration of the Holy Place.

V. THE PORTRAYAL OF THE ABOMINATION

In Revelation 13 is a graphic portrayal of the abomination of desolation. We meet the Antichrist, who is described in verse 1 as the beast. Verse 5 says, "There was given unto him a mouth speaking great things and blasphemies, and power was given unto him to continue forty and two months." Forty-two months equals 1260 days, or three-and-a-half years. Once again, as in Daniel, we see the Antichrist will flourish during the second half of the Tribulation. At the midpoint of the Tribulation, he starts to blaspheme God: "He opened his mouth in blasphemy against God, to blaspheme his name, and his tabernacle, and them that dwell in heaven" (v. 6).

Not only does the Antichrist blaspheme God, but verse 7 tells us that he also attacks the saints: "It was given unto him to make war with the saints, and to overcome them; and power was given him over all kindreds, and tongues and nations." Then in verse 8 we read of the abomination of desolation: "All that dwell upon the earth shall worship him." The Antichrist will set up an image of himself as the object of worldwide worship (v. 15). Verses 11-15 describe the work of the false prophet, who does great signs and wonders and brings the world to worship the image of the Antichrist.

Antiochus Epiphanes set up the image of a Greek god; the Antichrist will set up an image of himself. As Paul tells us in 2 Thessalonians 2:4, he will be the one who "exalteth himself above all that is called God, or that is worshiped, so that he, as God, sitteth in the temple of God, showing himself that he is God." The Antichrist will actually set himself up to be worshiped as God. That is the abomination of desolation.

Conclusion

What will drive Israel to rely upon the Antichrist? I believe it will be their fear of the Soviet Union and the Arabs. When I was in Israel I talked to some of the leaders, both military and civilian. They are afraid of the Arabs. They don't trust them because they know their hatred is so deep. They're also afraid of the Soviet Union, because whenever they capture weapons from the Arabs, they're always Soviet weapons. They know there is a Soviet-Arab alliance surrounding them.

During the end times the king of the north (Rosh—modern Russia) is going to come against Israel (Ezek. 38:2-3, NASB). Allied with the king of the north will be Persia (Ezek. 38:5). Ancient Persia basically occupied the territory of two modern nations: Iran and Afghanistan. Before the Soviet occupation of Afghanistan, it was difficult to see how that country fit into the picture, but now we know—Afghanistan is controlled by the Soviet Union. Ezekiel 38:5 also says that Put (modern Libya) will be allied with the king of the north. Libya's Colonel Qaddafi has obvious pro-Soviet leanings. Israel is surrounded by hostile nations allied with the Soviet Union.

Satanically Inspired Hatred

Islamic expert Lance Lambert says of Islam's hatred of Israel:

"Islam has at its very heart a dogmatic belief that it must triumph. . . . [Ultimately, those who] confess that Mohammed is not the Prophet and that the Koran is not the final word of God, they are worthy only of death. . . .

"Westerners cannot conceive of nations that base their whole policy and program on Islamic theology. But that is precisely what is happening [in] . . . Iran, Libya and Saudi Arabia. . . .

"It is the same thing that we witnessed in the rise of Fascism in Italy with Benito Mussolini, or the rise of National Socialism in Germany with Adolf Hitler . . . it is not just ideological, it is theological. . . . [Muslims] actually believe that their God has given them the oil weapon in order to finally win. . . .

"Can you not see that Israel is an affront to Islam? . . a Jewish nation, with a Jewish leadership [and] . . . army is an obscenity in the eyes of Islam.

"That is why the Bible says there will be war after war—all centered upon those few square meters of land where the Temple once stood, where now the Mosques of Omar and El-Aqsa stand.

"Is it not interesting that Syrian president Assad disarmed every PLO man that's gone into Syria. . . . They know they are producing terrorists for the subversion of the whole free world . . . in this little, beautiful land of Lebanon . . . the PLO established a worldwide base for terrorism.

"The KGB world center for terrorism has been in Beirut" (quoted in Dave Hunt, *Peace, Prosperity, and the Coming Holocaust* [Eugene, Oreg.: Harvest, 1983], p. 223).

We see that the Islamic world's hatred of Israel is not only political but also theological. Soldiers in Israel told me that if the Arabs believe Allah is telling them to kill Jews, they kill Jews. If someone like Khomeini should declare a holy war, treaties would mean nothing.

As we see the Soviet-Arab alliance growing, with its satanically inspired hatred of Israel, we know that the whole prophetic picture is coming together. Israel one day will try to neutralize that alliance by seeking protection from a man who also will turn out to be controlled by Satan. Just when Israel thinks they have found safety, he will betray them and set himself up as God. And that will unleash all the horrors of the Tribulation.

Focusing on the Facts

1. True or false: The Tribulation is a New Testament teaching not found in the Old Testament (see p. 64).
2. What does Isaiah tell us about the time just before the second coming of Christ (see p. 64)?
3. Jeremiah describes Israel's suffering in the end time as the time of _____ _____ (see p. 65).
4. What statistics does Zechariah give that indicate how severe Israel's suffering is going to be (see pp. 65-66)?
5. Why is the rapture not mentioned in Matthew 24 and 25 (see p. 66)?
6. How does Daniel describe the Antichrist in chapter 11 (see p. 66)?
7. When does the Antichrist commit the abomination of desolation (see p. 67)?
8. What is the abomination of desolation (see p. 67)?
9. Where will the abomination of desolation take place (see pp. 67-68)?
10. _____ _____ was a ruler of the second-century B.C. ruler who committed an act that pictures what the Antichrist will do in the end times (see p. 68).
11. True or false: The seventy weeks of years in Daniel 9 were completed at Jesus's triumphal entry into Jerusalem (see pp. 69-70).
12. What is the purpose of the thirty- and forty-five-day periods that follow the end of the Tribulation (see pp. 70-71)?
13. What event ushers in the worst period of the Tribulation (see p. 71)?
14. In what way will the Antichrist's desecration of the Temple be worse than what Antiochus Epiphanes did (see p. 72)?
15. What will motivate Israel to make an alliance with the Antichrist (see p. 72)?
16. Explain the prophetic significance of the Soviet Union's invasion of Afghanistan (see p. 72).

Pondering the Principles

1. During the Tribulation, the nation of Israel will put its trust in a man instead of the Lord—with disastrous results. What are some of the things you rely on, instead of trusting God, when

you go through times of struggle? According to the following verses, where should we place our trust in those times: Psalm 9:10; 40:4; 56:3-4, 11; 118:8-9; and Jeremiah 17:5, 7-8? Memorize at least one of these passages as a way of being prepared for the next struggle.

2. The abomination of desolation will be the worst incident of idolatry in all history. While few of us are tempted to worship a statue, we all tend to have idols of our own, such as our jobs, our marriages and families, our ministries, sports, hobbies, or anything else that becomes more important to us than our walk with the Lord. Looking back over the past week, what did you spend your time on? Did anything in your life take up more of your time than it should have? If so, spend some time this week examining your priorities and restructuring your schedule to reflect them.

5
Warnings of Coming Peril

Outline

Introduction

Lesson
I. Sudden Calamity (vv. 16-22)
   A. The Reaction to the Calamity
      1. The fugitives
      2. The fatalities
         a) Described in Zechariah
         b) Described in Revelation
      3. The friend
         a) His identity
         b) His intervention
      4. The forewarning
      5. The feeble
      6. The flight
   B. The Representation of the Calamity
   C. The Result of the Calamity
      1. Revelation 6
      2. Revelation 8
      3. Revelation 16
   D. Those Redeemed from the Calamity
      1. Their identification
      2. Their preservation
II. Subtle Confusion (vv. 23-27)
   A. Avoiding False Christs
      1. The enticement of the elect
      2. The protection of the elect
      3. The exhortation to the elect

B. Awaiting the True Christ
III. Sinful Corruption (v. 28)

Conclusion

Introduction

The second coming of Jesus Christ, both from the standpoint of warning unbelievers of the coming judgment and of encouraging believers with the promise of reward to come, is a highly motivating subject. The apostle Paul, realizing that Christ will come to judge unbelievers, says in 2 Corinthians 5:11, "Knowing, therefore, the terror of the Lord, we persuade men." Paul says in verse 9, "We labor that, whether present or absent, we may be accepted of him." We are to serve the Lord because we want to be found faithful at His return. Jesus describes His return in the Olivet discourse of Matthew 24-25.

Establishing Jesus' Prophetic Credentials

People sometimes wonder why Jesus predicted the destruction of the Temple since the Olivet discourse is a sermon about His second coming. There is an important reason: prophets often gave a short-range prophecy along with one for the distant future. When the short-range prophecy came true, it verified the credibility of the prophet and made his future prophecy believable. That Jesus predicted the destruction of Jerusalem in verse 2 does not indicate His whole sermon is on that topic, but His prediction does give a historical reference point to verify that He speaks the truth.

This prediction of Jesus was fulfilled in A.D. 70 when the Romans destroyed the Temple—not one stone was left upon another. Jesus predicted something that could never have been anticipated. None of the people of His day would have imagined that anyone would have the power or desire to destroy such a magnificent edifice—but that is exactly what happened. Since we know that Jesus' prediction of the Temple's destruction came to pass, we can believe His predictions regarding His second coming. Matthew 24:1-2 establishes Jesus' credentials as a truthful prophet.

Lesson

I. SUDDEN CALAMITY (vv. 16-22)

A. The Reaction to the Calamity

1. The fugitives

Jesus said that when the abomination of desolation is set up, "then let them who are in Judaea flee into the mountains" (v. 16). The Greek word translated "flee" is *pheugō*, from which we get the English word *fugitive*. As long as believers stay in Jerusalem, their lives will be in danger. The Jewish people especially will be targets of persecution, because the Antichrist wants to destroy Israel. That has always been Satan's plan, because if he can eliminate Israel, he can frustrate God's plan to save Israel and bring about the kingdom.

2. The fatalities

Not everyone who attempts to escape will get away. Several passages speak of the terrible slaughter of Jews and believing Gentiles during this time.

a) Described in Zechariah

Zechariah 13:8 says, "It shall come to pass that in all the land, saith the Lord, two parts in it shall be cut off and die; but the third shall be left in it." When the Antichrist moves against Israel, two out of three are going to die. The remaining third will be spared, refined, and kept by God (v. 9).

b) Described in Revelation

Revelation 6:9-11 tells us what takes place when the fifth seal is opened: "I saw under the altar the souls of them that were slain for the word of God, and for the testimony which they held. And they cried with a loud voice saying, How long, O Lord, holy and true, dost thou not judge and avenge our blood on them that dwell on the earth? And white robes were given unto every one of them; and it was said unto them that they should rest yet for a little season, until their fellow servants also and their brethren, that should be killed as they were, should be fulfilled." That passage describes believers of the Tribulation who have been martyred for their faith. They too did not escape the terrible onslaught of the Antichrist.

Other passages in Revelation describe the carnage of this time. Chapter 11 speaks of seven thousand people dying in the city of Jerusalem because of an earthquake (v. 13), and chapter 12 refers to martyrs who "loved not their lives unto the death" (v. 11). While some will deny Christ rather than die, others will sacrifice their lives for the testimony of Christ. In Revelation 13:7 we read that the Antichrist will make war with the Tribulation saints and overcome them. Chapter 17 pictures the false religious system as being drunk with the blood of the martyrs (v. 6).

3. The friend

   a) His identity

   Revelation 12 speaks of Michael, the angel whose special task is to protect Israel. He will provide supernatural help for those who manage to escape from the Antichrist. Chapter 12 describes a woman (Israel), her child (Christ), and a dragon (Satan). The dragon persecutes the woman and tries to kill the child. However, Michael comes to the aid of the woman and her child. Verses 7-8 describe Michael's defeat of Satan and his demonic forces.

   b) His intervention

   Verse 6 describes the flight of the woman (Israel) into the wilderness: "The woman fled into the wilderness, where she hath a place prepared by God, that they should feed her there a thousand two hundred and threescore days." After the Antichrist breaks his covenant with Israel at the midpoint of the Tribulation, the survivors flee and are hidden by God for 1260 days (three-and-a-half years).

Verse 14 reads, "To the woman were given two wings of a great eagle." I take that as a reference to Michael, the great protector of Israel, who will take them into the wilderness. There they will be nourished for "a time, and times, and half a time" (three-and-a-half years).

4. The forewarning

Matthew 24:17 says, "Let him who is on the housetop not come down to take anything out of his house." In ancient times the housetop was where the patio was. An outside staircase led up to it, and people would gather up there to relax. Jesus was warning any who happen to get caught up there not to even go inside the house to get their belongings, but to get down the stairs and out of town. Devastation and death will come as swiftly as a flash flood or a brush fire across the land—any delay will mean death. The Lord doesn't ask them to stay and face the bullets; He expects them to take normal precautions for their safety.

Verse 18 adds a further warning along the same lines: "Neither let him who is in the field return back to take his clothes." The Greek word translated "clothes" refers to the outer cloak. Jesus warns that the one working in the field who leaves his cloak somewhere else should not go back for it but flee immediately.

5. The feeble

Verse 19 warns that the weak and helpless will be especially vulnerable: "Woe unto those who are with child, and to those who nurse children in those days!" Why does our Lord single out pregnant women and nursing mothers for a special warning? Some commentators say it is because it will be hard for them to run, and that is true, but I believe Hosea 13 gives us another reason.

81

Verse 16 says, "Samaria shall become desolate; for she hath rebelled against her God. They shall fall by the sword; their infants shall be dashed in pieces, and their women with child shall be ripped up."

When Satan tried to stop the birth of Christ, he massacred the infants of Bethlehem. When Satan wanted to kill Moses, he slaughtered the Hebrew babies. And it won't be any different in the Tribulation. The Antichrist will bring upon the world such hellish atrocities that they will include infants being smashed to pieces and pregnant women being ripped open. I believe that is the primary reason for the Lord's warning in Matthew 24:19. That such things could happen seems unbelievable to us, but that's because we don't understand how terrible the holocaust will be when Satan has total control of the world.

6. The flight

Jesus says in verse 20, "Pray that your flight be not in the winter, neither on the sabbath day." Winter brings cold temperatures, rain, and in some parts of Israel, snow. All those things hamper attempts to travel swiftly.

The Lord also told them to pray that their flight may not be on the Sabbath. Even today ultra-orthodox Jews in Jerusalem will stone people who drive through their areas on the Sabbath. If the Jews were to flee on the Sabbath, that would be a great hindrance to their journey.

B. The Representation of the Calamity

Verse 21 says, "For then shall be great tribulation, such as was not since the beginning of the world to this time, no, nor ever shall be." The coming calamity will be the most severe holocaust of all human history. It is described in detail in Revelation 6-19, where the seal, trumpet, and bowl judgments indicate the escalating intensity of God's judgments on the earth. It should be noted that such a severe, worldwide calamity far exceeds the destruction of Jerusalem in A.D. 70.

C. The Result of the Calamity

Verse 22 gives a fascinating result of the calamity: "Except those days should be shortened, there should no flesh be saved; but for the elect's sake those days shall be shortened." There are a couple of ways to interpret the phrase "except those days should be shortened." There is no indication in Scripture that the three-and-a-half-year period of intense persecution will be shortened, so our Lord was not referring to that. Some have interpreted the Greek word translated "shortened" (ekolobōthēsan) to mean the Tribulation stops instantly. The word can have that meaning. Our Lord would then be saying that unless the holocaust ended quickly, even the elect would be devastated.

I believe there's a better interpretation of the phrase. Note Jesus used the plural, "those days." If He had used the singular, "that day," it would embrace the whole Tribulation period. "Day" is often used to denote a prophetic period of time (such as the "day of the Lord") rather than a twenty-four-hour period. Since the text says "those days," it seems best to assume that Jesus spoke of literal twenty-four-hour days. I believe that when the abomination of desolation occurs and people start running for their lives, God will supernaturally shorten the length of daylight to give them the protection of darkness. There are three passages in Revelation that support this understanding of verse 22:

1. Revelation 6

Verses 12-14 describe the events that take place after the sixth seal is opened: "There was a great earthquake, and the sun became black as sackcloth of hair, and the moon became like blood; and the stars of heaven fell unto the earth, even as a fig tree casteth her untimely figs, when she is shaken of a mighty wind. And the heaven departed as a scroll when it is rolled together; and every mountain and island were moved out of their places." That passage describes a drastic alteration of the heavenly bodies. If the sun, moon, and stars go out, the result will be darkness.

2. Revelation 8

Verse 12 records the fourth of the trumpet judgments: "The third part of the sun was smitten, and the third part of the moon, and the third part of the stars, so that the third part of them was darkened, and the day shown not for a third part of it." That passage indicates daylight will be reduced by a third.

3. Revelation 16

This chapter describes all the bowl judgments. Verse 10 says this about the fifth bowl of wrath: "The fifth angel poured out his bowl upon the throne of the beast, and his kingdom was full of darkness; and they gnawed their tongues for pain." As the Tribulation goes on, the daylight gradually diminishes until at the end there is total darkness. That is a protection for the elect.

D. Those Redeemed from the Calamity

1. Their identification

"Elect" in Matthew 24:22 is primarily a reference to Israel, though it also encompasses the Gentiles who will be saved during the Tribulation. Israel is referred to in the Old Testament as God's elect (e.g., Isa. 42:1). God will protect His people. He will spare one third so that He can redeem them and bring them into the kingdom. Jesus here is referring to Israel as a nation, as Paul does in Romans 9-11. That is the first usage of the word *elect* in the New Testament, and it introduces a new truth about those who belong to God—we belong to Him because He chose us. The Greek word translated "elect" (*eklegō*) means "to choose" or "to call out." There's no question that God chose Israel; even those who deny the doctrine of election as it relates to individuals seldom deny God's election of Israel. The nation as a whole, and individual believers as well, are chosen by God.

2. Their preservation

If it weren't for God's care of His elect, no one would survive the holocaust of the Tribulation. There would be no redeemed Jews or Gentiles to go into the kingdom. That illustrates a marvelous truth: when God chooses someone for Himself, He will protect that person even if He has to restructure the entire universe to do it. What a comforting thought!

II. SUBTLE CONFUSION (vv. 23-27)

After the abomination of desolation is set up, believers will flee. Although many will die, some will survive and be protected by the Lord. They will understand from their reading of Matthew that the events having just taken place indicate the second coming is imminent. That, coupled with their desperate circumstances, will make them vulnerable to false rumors that Christ has returned.

A. Avoiding False Christs

1. The enticement of the elect

   Verse 23 says, "If any man shall say unto you, Lo, here is Christ, or there; believe it not." Satan will try to trick the elect into coming out of hiding so he can kill them. Not only will there be rumors that the true Christ has returned, but there will arise false christs who will "show great signs and wonders" (v. 24). They'll do things that are so clever they would deceive even the elect, if that were possible.

2. The protection of the elect

   Those who are truly elect could never be deceived about who Christ is because our Lord says in verse 24, "*If* it were possible" (emphasis added). That means it is not possible to deceive the elect. Jesus says in John 10:27, "My sheep hear my voice, and I know them, and they follow me." Anyone who follows a false christ proves that he never knew the true Christ. Once you know the true Christ you can't be fooled.

3. The exhortation to the elect

   Verse 25 reads, "Behold, I have told you before." This is not the first time Jesus has warned of the danger of false christs or false prophets. Earlier in the Olivet discourse, He warned of them (Matt. 24:5, 11) as He did throughout His ministry (cf. Matt. 7:15-20; 15:7-9, 13-14; 16:6-12; 23:1-12). Verse 26 says not to believe it if someone says to you, "He's in the desert," or, "We've got Him hidden in a secret chamber."

B. Awaiting the True Christ

The second coming of the true Christ will be unmistakable. Verse 27 describes it this way: "As the lightning cometh out of the east, and shineth even unto the west, so shall also the coming of the Son of man be." Christ's coming will be sudden and glorious, and the whole world is going to see it. Revelation 1:7 says, "Behold, he cometh with clouds, and every eye shall see him." Christ's coming will not be quiet or secret.

Revelation 19:11-16 gives a vivid description of Christ's return. He will come out of heaven riding on a white horse, accompanied by the saints and angels in all the glory of heaven. He will come with a sword in His hand, wearing a blood-spattered garment, to bring judgment on the world and destroy all the armies who have come against Him in battle. Revelation 6:15-17 tells us the people of the world will cry for the rocks and the mountains to hide them from the face of His glory when they see Him coming. Christ's second coming will be devastating, and the whole world will know when He comes.

III. SINFUL CORRUPTION (v. 28)

Verse 28 gives another reason for true believers to flee: "Wherever the carcass is, there will the eagles be gathered together." That proverb shows how corrupt the world will become after the Antichrist shows his true colors.

The Greek word translated "eagles" (*aetoi*) could be better translated "vultures" in this context. The world is going to be so sinfully corrupt that it will be like a decaying carcass with vultures hovering around. Jesus will come in judgment to tear that carcass to pieces. That is a vivid picture. Jesus tells us in verse 12 that "iniquity shall abound." Paul had that scene in mind when he wrote that Jesus will return "in flaming fire taking vengeance on them that know not God, and that obey not the gospel of our Lord Jesus Christ" (2 Thess. 1:8).

Conclusion

What does Jesus tell those who are alive when the abomination of desolation occurs to do? He warns them to flee from sudden calamity, beware of subtle confusion, and avoid the sinful corruption of the world, which will ultimately be judged at the second coming of our Lord Jesus Christ.

Focusing on the Facts

1. Why is the second coming a source of motivation for unbelievers (see p. 78)?
2. Why is the second coming a source of motivation for believers (see p. 78)?
3. Explain in your own words why Jesus predicted the destruction of the Temple in A.D. 70 since His sermon is about the second coming (see p. 78).
4. What special danger will Jewish people face from the Antichrist (see p. 79)?
5. According to Zechariah 13:8, _____ _____ of the Jewish people who flee will be killed (see p. 79).
6. _____ is the angel whose special task is the protection of Israel (see p. 80).
7. What special peril will pregnant women and nursing mothers face (see pp. 81-82)?
8. How would the Sabbath hinder the flight of the Jewish people (see p. 82)?
9. According to Matthew 24:22, what will be shortened to protect God's people? Give biblical support for your answer (see p. 83).
10. Who are the elect referred to in Matthew 24:22 (see p. 84)?
11. What are some reasons the elect might be susceptible to satanic deception (see p. 85)?
12. List some of the other occasions in Jesus' ministry when He warned against false prophets (see pp. 85-86).

Pondering the Principles

1. One of the proofs that Jesus Christ is who He claimed to be is that prophecies He made have been fulfilled. Another proof is that He fulfilled prophecies made about Him in the Old Testament. Match the Old Testament prophecy with the New Testament passage describing its fulfillment:

   a. Isaiah 7:14   1. Matthew 2:1
   b. Micah 5:2   2. Luke 23:33
   c. Zechariah 9:9   3. John 19:23-24
   d. Psalm 22:16   4. Matthew 1:18-25
   e. Isaiah 53:9   5. Luke 19:35-37
   f. Zechariah 11:12   6. Matthew 27:57-60
   g. Psalm 22:18   7. Matthew 26:15

2. In the midst of the greatest holocaust the world will ever know, God will show His care for His people by shortening the days to protect them. Meditate on the following psalms, and praise God for His care for you: Psalms 27, 34, and 91. What has been your reaction to trials in the past? What have you learned from these passages to help you better handle difficult situations in the future?

6
The Sign of the Son of Man

Outline

Introduction

Lesson
I. The Sequence of the Events
II. The Scene in the Heavens
   A. As Described by Matthew
   B. As Described by the Old Testament Prophets
     1. In Isaiah 13
     2. In Isaiah 34
     3. In Joel 2
III. The Sign in the Sky
   A. The Definition of the Sign
     1. What it is not
       a) The sign of the cross
       b) The *Shekinah* alone
     2. What it is
   B. The Description of the Sign
     1. The previews
     2. The particulars
       a) Clouds
       b) Light
IV. The Strength of the Lord
   A. To Judge the Wicked
   B. To Restore the Earth
V. The Sorrow of Israel
VI. The Selection by the Angels

Conclusion

Introduction

Those of us who know the Lord and study His Word are aware that man's dominion over the world will end with the glorious return of Jesus Christ. The first time He came, He came to die on a cross, but He will return to reign as King of kings and Lord of lords. After Christ ascended into heaven, two angels said to the disciples, "This same Jesus, who is taken up from you into heaven, shall so come in like manner as ye have seen him go into heaven" (Acts 1:11). Jesus will return bodily, just the way He went away.

Throughout all the history of the church, believers have looked for the coming of the Lord Jesus Christ. The apostle Paul writes in Titus 2:11-14, "The grace of God that bringeth salvation hath appeared to all men, teaching us that, denying ungodliness and worldly lusts, we should live soberly, righteously, and godly, in this present age, looking for that blessed hope, and the glorious appearing of the great God and our Savior, Jesus Christ, who gave himself for us that he might redeem us from all iniquity, and purify unto himself a people of his own, zealous of good works." The hope of Christ's return should motivate us to live holy, obedient lives, for when He returns, our bodies will be changed and made like His glorious body (Phil. 3:21).

The world is familiar with the details of Christ's first coming, but it is far less familiar with the circumstances of His second coming. In Matthew 24:29-31, our Lord describes the very moment of His second coming.

Lesson

I. THE SEQUENCE OF THE EVENTS

Verse 29 tells us where the second coming fits into the chronology of end-time events: "Immediately after the tribulation of those days." That verse in its context clearly states the second coming will immediately follow the time period called the Tribulation.

"Tribulation" (Gk., *thlipsis*) means "trouble," "difficulty," or "distress." To make clear what tribulation He was talking about, Jesus describes it as "the tribulation of those days." That refers to the days He describes in verses 4-28. Note especially verse 21: "For then shall be great tribulation, such as was not since the beginning of the world to this time, no, nor ever shall be." The Tribulation Jesus referred to is the worst the world will ever know—the period of intense trouble that will follow the abomination of desolation.

II. THE SCENE IN THE HEAVENS

In verse 29 the Lord sets the stage for the second coming: "The sun [shall] be darkened, and the moon shall not give its light, and the stars shall fall from heaven, and the powers of the heavens shall be shaken." Just before the Lord appears, the universe will begin to disintegrate. Luke 21:25-26, a parallel passage to verse 29, adds more details: "There shall be signs in the sun, and in the moon, and in the stars; and upon the earth distress of nations, with perplexity; the sea and the waves roaring; men's hearts failing them for fear, and for looking after those things which are coming on the earth; for the powers of heaven shall be shaken." Luke tells us there will be signs on earth as well as in the heavens—signs so dramatic and cataclysmic that men's hearts will fail them. The Greek word translated "failing" in verse 26 (*apopsuchontōn*) actually means "to expire." People will die from terror.

A. As Described by Matthew

Matthew 24:29 tells us, "The powers of the heavens shall be shaken." Everything in the universe is held together by the power of God (Heb. 1:3). He prevents orbits from fluctuating. We can navigate our spacecraft with accuracy to distant planets because of the unchanging, fixed powers of the heavens. The heavenly bodies move consistently at all times and do what they are predicted to do. Scientists can even mathematically predict what heavenly bodies will do thousands of years in the future because of the uniformity of the past.

Just before the second coming, the Lord will relax the powers that normally hold the universe together, bringing about chaos. Heavenly bodies will career at random through space as the earth becomes a victim of this cosmic breakdown.

Specifically, Jesus said that the sun will go black. The implications of that are staggering—man can't survive for long without sunlight. There would also be dramatic temperature changes. Jesus said the moon won't give its light, since its light is reflected from the sun. The changes in the heavens will cause the tides to be erratic. Revelation 6:13-14 says the stars will fall like overripe figs off a fig tree, and the heavens will be rolled up like a scroll.

Only divine intervention will prevent the extinction of life until the establishment of the kingdom.

B. As Described by the Old Testament Prophets

1. In Isaiah 13

Many people believe Isaiah 13 relates only to Babylon's destruction, but I believe it has a broader reference than that. Note that the Hebrew word translated "land" (*erets*) in verse 9 should be translated "earth" in this context. Also, verse 11 speaks of God's punishing the world, not just Babylon. Isaiah 13 does predict Babylon's destruction, but, as often happens in prophecy, there is a short-range prediction that typifies another prediction for the distant future. Isaiah sees in the destruction of Babylon a microcosm of what will happen in the world at the second coming of the Lord.

Verses 6-16 describe the coming judgment: "Wail; for the day of the Lord is at hand; it shall come as a destruction from the Almighty. Therefore shall all hands be faint, and every man's heart shall melt; and they shall be afraid. Pangs and sorrows shall take hold of them; they shall be in pain like a woman that travaileth. They shall be amazed one at another; their faces shall be as flames. Behold, the day of the Lord cometh, cruel both with wrath and fierce anger, to lay the land desolate; and he shall destroy the sinners out of it. For the stars of heaven and the constellations thereof shall not give their light; the sun shall be darkened in its going forth, and the moon shall not cause its light to shine. And I will punish the world for its evil, and the wicked for their iniquity; and I will cause the arrogancy of the proud to cease, and will lay low the haughtiness of the terrible. I will make a man more rare than fine gold, even a man than the golden wedge of Ophir. Therefore, I will shake the heavens, and the earth shall remove out of its place, in the wrath of the Lord of hosts, and in the day of his fierce anger. And it shall be like the chased roe, and like a sheep that no man taketh up; they shall every man turn to his own people, and flee everyone into his own land. Every one that is found shall be thrust through, and every one that is joined unto them shall fall by the sword. Their children also shall be dashed to pieces before their eyes; their houses shall be spoiled, and their wives ravished."

Isaiah predicted a terrible time of judgment. Men will die on account of God's terrible judgment (v. 7), and there will be worldwide slaughter to the point that men themselves become as rare as gold (v. 12). There will be signs in the heavens and on earth—just as our Lord taught in the Olivet discourse.

2. In Isaiah 34

Isaiah again looks into the distant future and says in verses 1-4, "Come near, ye nations, to hear; and hearken, ye peoples: let the earth hear, and all that is therein; the world, and all things that come forth from it. For the indignation of the Lord is upon all nations, and his fury upon all their armies; he hath utterly destroyed them, he hath delivered them to the slaughter. Their slain also shall be cast out, and their stench shall come up out of their carcasses, and the mountains shall be melted with their blood. And all the host of heaven shall be dissolved, and the heavens shall be rolled together like a scroll; and all their host shall fall down, as the leaf falleth off from the vine, and like a falling fig from the fig tree."

Once again it is clear from verse 2 that Isaiah is referring to the judgment of the world, not one particular nation. He predicts the great slaughter that will ensue when God destroys the armies gathered against Jerusalem at the battle of Armageddon (v. 2).

Isaiah goes on to say in verse 6, "The sword of the Lord is filled with blood; it is made fat with fatness, and with the blood of lambs and goats, with the fat of the kidneys of rams; for the Lord hath a sacrifice in Bozrah, and a great slaughter in the land of Edom." Bozrah was the main city of Edom. It will be the southern border of the battle of Armageddon. Revelation 14:20 tells us the battle of Armageddon will cover an area of sixteen hundred furlongs, or two hundred miles. If you measure two hundred miles to the north, starting with Bozrah, it takes you just past Armageddon into Lebanon. That is the extent of the battle of Armageddon. The Bible is accurate in describing what verse 8 calls "the day of the Lord's vengeance and the year of recompenses"—the day when God pays back sinful man.

3. In Joel 2

Joel describes a locust swarm that blots out the sun and moon. It seemed to him that the earth shuddered as they landed on the ground (v. 10). He used that as an illustration of the ultimate shaking of the heavens and the earth as a result of divine judgment (vv. 30-31).

Haggai described the coming judgment in the same terms (Hag. 2:6-7). Peter, preaching on the Day of Pentecost, quoted the prophecy of Joel that the day will come when the sun goes dark and the moon turns to blood—all those things are part of this coming holocaust.

Canceling the Curse

Romans 8:19-22 says the whole creation waits for the glorious manifestation of the children of God. When the Lord appears, the corrupt universe will be replaced by a purified and recreated universe that will be all that God ever intended it to be. All of creation groans, waiting for that reality. Scripture speaks often of the day when the Lord will tear down what is in order to put up what ought to be.

III. THE SIGN IN THE SKY

In Matthew 24:30 Jesus answers the question the disciples asked Him previously: "What shall be the sign of thy coming, and of the end of the age?" (v. 3). He gave them a list of general signs (vv. 4-14), but He still hadn't given them *the* sign.

A. The Definition of the Sign

1. What it is not

   a) The sign of the cross

   Some early church Fathers taught that the sign of which Christ spoke was a blazing cross that would fill the black heavens. This was the position of men such as Chrysostom, Cyril of Jerusalem, and Origen.

   b) The *Shekinah* alone

   Others have taught that the sign will be the *Shekinah*—the blazing light of God's glory. That's closer to the truth, but you can't have the *Shekinah* apart from the One it emanates from.

2. What it is

   Verse 30 defines what the sign will be: "Then shall appear the sign of the Son of man in heaven." That is a subjective genitive in the Greek text, indicating that the sign is the Son of Man Himself. In the midst of the blackness will appear in blazing, unveiled glory the Son of Man.

B. The Description of the Sign

1. The previews

   The Bible records several instances when men received a glimpse of God's glory. In Matthew 17 Jesus took James, Peter, and John up a mountain, pulled aside the veil of His flesh, and showed them His glory; they got a taste of His second coming appearance. Adam had a glimpse of it in the Garden when he walked in the cool of the day with the presence of God. The people of Israel had a glimpse of God's glory when it dwelt between the wings of the cherubim in the Holy of Holies. They saw it as a cloud that led them by day and a fire that led them by night. But the world has never seen the full, unveiled glory that Christ will reveal at His second coming, and they will scream for mercy and cry for the rocks and the mountains to cover them, lest they be consumed by it (Rev. 6:15-17).

2. The particulars

   a) Clouds

   The end of verse 30 tells us that Jesus will come on the clouds of heaven. Just as He ascended into heaven on clouds, so He will return in the same manner (Acts 1:9-11). Daniel (Dan. 7:13), John (Rev. 1:7), Mark (Mark 13:26), Luke (Luke 21:27), and Matthew all say He will come on the clouds of heaven (Matt. 24:30; 26:64).

   The Old Testament tells us that clouds are the chariot of God. Psalm 104:1, 3 says, "Bless the Lord, O my soul. O Lord my God, thou art very great; thou art clothed with honor and majesty . . . who layeth the beams of his chambers in the waters; who maketh the clouds his chariot, who walketh upon the wings of the wind." Isaiah 19:1 says, "The Lord rideth upon a swift cloud."

   b) Light

   Zechariah 14:6-7 describes the blazing light that will accompany Christ's return. Verse 6 can be translated, "It shall be in that day that there shall not be light, the glorious ones will wane," or, "The bright ones will fade." Either way it refers to the stars, the sun, and the moon. All the lights in the sky will go out. Verse 7 says, "It shall be one day which shall be known to the Lord." It is one day that only the Lord could explain.

Zechariah goes on to say in verse 7, "Not day and not night." Since the sun, moon, and stars have waned, there can't be day or night as we know them. He continues, "It will be at the time of closing, the time of evening, the time of the end of that day, there will be light." The light accompanying Christ when He returns will bring an abrupt end to the darkness of the Tribulation.

Revelation 21:23 and 22:5 give us some idea of the brightness of the light. Those passages tell us that in the New Jerusalem, there will be no lamp or sunlight, because the Lord Himself will light it up.

The Church Has a Front-Row Seat

Some people wonder where the church will be while all those things are happening. I believe the church will be raptured before the Tribulation begins (cf. 1 Thess. 1:10; Rev. 3:10). Believers will be participating in the marriage supper of the Lamb, where they'll get their rewards (cf. 1 Cor. 3:11-15; 2 Cor. 5:10). Does that mean they won't get to see Christ's return? No. Colossians 3:4 says, "When Christ, who is our life, shall appear, then shall ye also appear with him in glory."

Revelation 19:7-8 describes the marriage supper of the Lamb, where the Lord is joined to His redeemed church, His bride. When the wife (the church) comes into the presence of the Lord, to her it is "granted that she should be arrayed in fine linen, clean and white; for the fine linen is the righteousness of saints" (v. 8).

John tells us in verse 14 that believers will return with Christ at His second coming: "The armies that were in heaven [the church and the Old Testament saints] followed him upon white horses, clothed in fine linen, white and clean." Believers will each have his own robe and his own white horse. They'll be there, only they'll be coming down with Christ, not on earth looking up at Him.

IV. THE STRENGTH OF THE LORD

Matthew 24:30 says Jesus will return "with power." It will take tremendous power to set the universe reeling and the earth rocking on its axis. He has power over all creation. He has power over Satan. He has power over demons. He has power to slaughter all Christ-rejecting unbelievers. He has power to establish His kingdom. And He has power to redeem His elect. That is power without equal.

A. To Judge the Wicked

Zechariah 14:4 tells us Christ will return to the very place He left—the Mount of Olives. According to Revelation 19, He will destroy many and will subject the survivors to the sheep-and-goat judgment (Matt. 25:31-46). Then He will establish His kingdom.

B. To Restore the Earth

Zechariah 14 describes some of the changes the Lord will make on the earth when He returns. Verse 8 says there will be a channel cut between the sea in front of the Mount of Olives (the Mediterranean) and the sea behind it (the Dead Sea). When I was in Israel, I was told the Israelis are trying to dig a channel or build a pipeline to bring water from the Mediterranean to the desert. The Lord will accomplish that when He returns, and the desert will then blossom like a rose (Isa. 35:1).

The canal from the Mediterranean to the desert is just one manifestation of the Lord's power to restore the earth. The book of Isaiah mentions these things in addition: the wolf will lie down with the lamb (Isa. 11:6), children will play with poisonous snakes and not be bitten (Isa. 11:8), and people will live long lives (Isa. 65:20).

V. THE SORROW OF ISRAEL

The Jewish nation will mourn at Christ's return. Zechariah 12:10 tells us "they shall look upon [Christ] whom they have pierced, and they shall mourn for him, as one mourneth for his only son." They will mourn that they have crucified their Messiah. Zechariah 13:1 says that when they do that, a fountain of cleansing will be opened to them. I believe it is at that moment when all Israel will be saved (cf. Rom. 11:26).

VI. THE SELECTION BY THE ANGELS

In verse 31 our Lord tells us angels will be used by God to gather men in the end times: "He shall send his angels with a great sound of a trumpet, and they shall gather together his elect from the four winds, from one end of heaven to the other." In the parables of Matthew 13, our Lord speaks of angels being sent out to gather people for judgment (v. 41). In Matthew 24:31, however, they're not gathering unbelievers for judgment but the elect for glory. Sounding a trumpet was the familiar Jewish way of calling an assembly. When the trumpet is blown, the angels gather God's elect from their hiding places.

"From the four winds" is a colloquial expression similar to "from the four corners of the world"—it's another way of saying from everywhere. None of the elect will miss the kingdom; the godly survivors of the Tribulation will enter it with the Old Testament saints (who are resurrected at this time).

Conclusion

Matthew 24:29-31 is the Lord's own description of the very moment of His second coming. Are you ready for His return? Will you be one of those who return with Him in glory, or will you miss out on His kingdom and be sent to an everlasting hell? Your eternal destiny is at stake. I pray you respond to the Savior.

Focusing on the Facts

1. Name a verse that indicates Christ's return will be a physical, bodily one (see p. 90).
2. Why should the second coming motivate us to live holy lives (see p. 90)?
3. When will the Tribulation Jesus refers to in Matthew 24:29 take place (see pp. 90-91)?
4. Will the signs associated with the return of Christ occur in the heavens only, or will there be signs on the earth as well (see p. 91)?

5. What will happen when the Lord relaxes the powers of the heavens (see pp. 91-92)?
6. Does Isaiah 13 refer only to the destruction of Babylon? Support your answer from Scripture (see p. 92).
7. What does the cursed creation await (see Rom. 8:19-22; p. 94)?
8. What are two things the sign of the Son of Man is not (see p. 95)?
9. Describe two particulars associated with Christ's return (see pp. 96-97).
10. What will the church be doing during the Tribulation (see p. 97)?
11. Will the church return with Christ at His second coming? Support your answer with Scripture (see p. 97).
12. To what spot will Christ return when He comes back to the earth (see p. 98)?
13. Describe some of the changes the Lord will make in the earth after His return (see p. 98).
14. Why will Israel mourn when Christ returns (see p. 98)?
15. Who will the angels gather at the second coming (see p. 99)?

Pondering the Principles

1. When Christ returns in judgment, the manifestation of His glory will be so terrifying that unbelievers will cry for the mountains and rocks to fall on them to hide them from God's wrath (Rev. 6:15-17). The apostle Paul said in 2 Corinthians 5:11, "Knowing, therefore, the terror of the Lord, we persuade men." How will the knowledge of the coming judgment affect your attitude toward the unsaved people in your life? Is there someone you have put off speaking to about Christ? Ask God to give you an opportunity to witness to an unsaved friend or loved one today.

2. Do you live in the light of eternity? Philippians 3:20-21 tells us Christ will change our bodies into glorious bodies like His. Colossians 3:4 says, "When Christ, who is our life, shall appear, then shall ye also appear with him in glory." How should knowing that affect how you view suffering in your life? Paul tells us in 2 Corinthians 4:17 that our afflictions are temporary and will bring us eternal glory. Memorize that verse and use it the next time you encounter trials in your life to keep them in perspective.

7
The Imminence of Christ's Return

Outline

Introduction

Lesson
I. An Uncomplicated Analogy (v. 32)
   A. The Exhortation
   B. The Examination
      1. The picture
      2. The principle
II. An Unmistakable Application (vv. 33-34)
   A. The Parallel (v. 33)
      1. How will we know when Christ's return is imminent?
      2. What will be near when Christ's return is imminent?
   B. The Promise (v. 34)
      1. The composition
         a) Who the generation isn't
            (1) The disciples
               (a) The Jesus-was-wrong theory
               (b) The A.D. 70 theory
            (2) The Jewish race
            (3) Those who reject Christ
            (4) The nation of Israel
         b) Who the generation is
      2. The chronology
         a) The post-Tribulation view
         b) The pre-Tribulation view
III. An Unchanging Authority (v. 35)

Introduction

The great hope of every Christian is the second coming of Jesus Christ. The Bible says believers are those who love His appearing (2 Tim. 4:8). Believers look "for that blessed hope, and the glorious appearing of the great God and our Savior, Jesus Christ" (Titus 2:13). Paul said they eagerly await "the glory which shall be revealed in us" (Rom. 8:18), "the glorious liberty of the children of God" (Rom. 8:19, 21), "the redemption of our body" (Rom. 8:23), and the coming of our Lord Jesus Christ (1 Cor. 1:7). Every believer looks forward to the day when the saints will judge the world (1 Cor. 6:2). We will all be changed (1 Cor. 15:51), and death will be forever defeated along with sin (1 Cor. 15:54). Someday we will be presented as a chaste virgin to Christ, who is our bridegroom (2 Cor. 11:2). We long for the day when we shall be absent from the body and present with the Lord (2 Cor. 5:8). When He appears, we will be like Him, for we will see Him as He is (1 John 3:2).

The theme of the second coming permeates the New Testament. Souls of believers are redeemed at the cross, and they look forward to the second coming, when their bodies will be redeemed and they enter into the fullness of their salvation. When Christ returns, Satan will be defeated. The curse will be lifted. All the saints will be glorified, Christ will be worshiped, and creation will be liberated. Sin and death will be conquered. The Lord's second coming is a real event that will take place in history just as His first coming did.

There are many passages of Scripture that discuss the Lord's second coming, but Matthew 24-25 is without equal because it's Jesus' own sermon on His return. So far we have learned about the signs that will precede the second coming and about the abomination of desolation. Jesus knew that the disciples were wondering about how much time would pass between the beginning of the birth pains to when He establishes His kingdom on earth. So to summarize what He had just said and make a transition to answering the disciples' next question, He gave the parable of the fig tree (Matt. 24:32-35).

The Purpose of Parables

In Matthew 13:10 the disciples ask Jesus, "Why speakest thou unto them in parables?" He answers in verse 11, "Because it is given

102

unto you to know the mysteries of the kingdom of heaven, but to them [the Jewish religious leaders and the multitudes] it is not given." Thus parables have a twofold purpose: when they are not explained they veil certain truths, and when they are explained they make those truths clear. As Jesus Himself said, parables hide things from the wise and prudent of this world and reveal them to babes (Luke 10:21).

Once you recognize that Jesus spoke in parables to enhance the disciples' understanding and not to confuse them, then you also realize that they aren't difficult to understand. Jesus used them to teach simple truths. You don't need to have a special study Bible or go to seminary to decipher parables. The disciples didn't have much to go on when they heard the parables, and you can understand them just as they did. That's especially important to know for the parable of the fig tree because it's frequently interpreted as an obscure allegory as opposed to a straightforward analogy. Our Lord didn't intend to complicate the disciples' understanding of the truths about His return.

Lesson

I. AN UNCOMPLICATED ANALOGY (v. 32)

"Now learn a parable of the fig tree: When its branch is yet tender, and putteth forth leaves, ye know that summer is near."

An analogy using a fig tree was easy for the disciples to understand. Fig trees were around them everywhere. In fact, earlier that morning Jesus had taught the disciples a lesson by using a fig tree (Matt. 21:18-22). The Lord saw a fig tree with leaves but no fruit and taught the disciples about fruitlessness and prayer.

Christ wasn't the first teacher to use a fig tree in His teaching. Jotham the son of Gideon uses a fig tree to illustrate a point in Judges 9:10-11. In Hosea 9:10, figs are used to speak of the patriarchs. Jeremiah used baskets of figs to speak of good and bad people (Jer. 24:2). Joel 1:7 uses a fig tree to teach a spiritual lesson. In the book of Revelation we read that during the Tribulation the heavens will collapse just as figs fall from a fig tree when a strong wind blows (Rev. 6:13). So the Israelites' familiarity with the fig tree made it ideal for illustrative purposes.

A. The Exhortation

Notice that when Jesus taught the parable of the fig tree, He began by saying, "Now *learn* a parable" (emphasis added). He wanted the disciples to get the point of His analogy. The Greek word translated "learn" (*manthanō*) speaks of learning something thoroughly—of acquiring a habit. Paul used a form of that word in Philippians 4:11, where he said, "I have learned, in whatever state I am, in this to be content." He didn't learn about contentment on a superficial level; it became ingrained in his life. Likewise, Jesus wanted the disciples to fully grasp the lesson He was teaching in the parable of the fig tree.

B. The Examination

In Matthew 24:32 Jesus says, "Now learn a parable of the fig tree: When its branch is yet tender, and putteth forth leaves, ye know that summer is near." When the tree first buds, you know it's spring. That means its almost time to harvest the fruit.

1. The picture

"When its branch is yet tender" refers to when the sap in the tree begins to flow through the branches at springtime, causing them to become tender and swollen. The new life pulsating through the branches produces buds that will become fruit. And because the branches are tender, the tree needs to be cared for. So Jesus was saying that when spring comes, that means summer is near, and summer is harvest time.

2. The principle

Whenever Christ speaks about harvests in the New Testament, He refers to the time when He will return to separate the good from the bad—when He returns to the earth in judgment. John the Baptist said, "I, indeed, baptize you with water unto repentance, but he who cometh after me [Christ] is mightier than I, whose shoes I am not worthy to bear; he shall baptize you with the Holy Spirit, and with fire" (Matt. 3:11). The fire refers to judgment. In the previous verse we read that any tree that doesn't bring forth good fruit will be cast into the fire. Verse 12 adds that Christ will sift the good from the bad just as wheat is sifted from chaff, and the bad (the chaff) will be burned with unquenchable fire.

In Matthew 9:36, we read that the Lord was moved with compassion when He looked upon the multitude, seeing they "were faint, and were scattered abroad, as sheep having no shepherd." He said, "The harvest truly is plenteous, but the laborers are few. Pray ye, therefore, the Lord of the harvest, that he will send forth laborers into his harvest" (vv. 37-38). Jesus saw the world as a harvest, knowing that one day God would bring judgment upon men. And He desired that some people would be sent into the world to warn men of God's impending judgment.

In the parable of the wheat and the tares, Jesus taught that the tares (false believers) are to be allowed to grow with the wheat (true believers) until the harvest—the time of judgment. He said, "In the time of harvest I will say to the reapers, Gather together first the tares, and bind them in bundles to burn them, but gather the wheat into my barn. . . . As, therefore, the tares are gathered and burned in the fire, so shall it be in the end of this age. The Son of man shall send forth his angels, and they shall gather out of his kingdom all things that offend, and them who do iniquity, and shall cast them into a furnace of fire; there shall be wailing and gnashing of teeth" (Matt. 13:30, 40-42).

So in the analogy of the fig tree, when Jesus said harvest was near, the disciples knew what He was talking about.

II. AN UNMISTAKABLE APPLICATION (vv. 33-34)

A. The Parallel (v. 33)

"So likewise ye, when ye shall see all these things, know that it is near, even at the doors."

The phrase "so likewise ye" linked the parable to the application Christ was about to present. Just as summer is imminent when a fig tree shoots forth leaves, so is the second coming imminent when the disciples "see all these things."

1. How will we know when Christ's return is imminent?

   "All these things" refers to everything Christ just talked about: the birth pains in verses 4-14, the abomination of desolation in verse 15, the need to flee because of the Great Tribulation in verses 16-28, and the stellar events of verses 29-31. All those things will signal the nearness of Christ's return, just as a tree with new shoots signifies that summer is coming.

2. What will be near when Christ's return is imminent?

   Jesus was referring specifically to God's kingdom when He said, "When ye shall see all these things, know that *it* is near" (emphasis added; cf. Luke 21:31). When man's age comes to an end, the kingdom of Jesus Christ will be established on this earth. The millennial kingdom of Revelation 20:4-5 will become a reality. Christ will reign with His redeemed saints for a thousand years on the earth. Satan will be bound during that time. Israel will be preserved from her enemies and become servant to the most high God. Zechariah 8:23 says, "In those days . . . ten men shall take hold out of all languages of the nations, even shall take hold of the skirt of him that is a Jew, saying, We will go with you; for we have heard that God is with you." Gentiles will seek the true God in the millennial kingdom.

Jesus ends verse 33 by saying, "Know that it is near, even at the doors." That's how close His return will be—so near that it's as if He were knocking on a door about to be opened.

B. The Promise (v. 34)

   "Verily I say unto you, This generation shall not pass, till all these things be fulfilled."

What generation was Jesus talking about? Which generation will not die off before all the events of Matthew 24 come to pass? Various theologians throughout the ages have offered many different answers.

1. The composition

  a) Who the generation isn't

   (1) The disciples

     (*a*) The Jesus-was-wrong theory

> Some people think Jesus was saying, "You disciples will not die before the second coming." But that couldn't be what the Lord was saying because all the disciples have been long dead, and Jesus has not yet returned. Those who say "this generation" refers to the disciples believe Jesus was wrong. They say Jesus obviously didn't know everything because He said, "That day and that hour knoweth no man, no, not the angels who are in heaven, neither the Son, but the Father" (Mark 13:32).

> What Jesus is really saying in Mark 13:32 is that in His incarnation—in becoming God in human flesh—He chose not to know when the second coming would be. It's one thing to choose not to know something and another to say something that's not true. In His incarnation, Jesus may have restricted His knowledge, but He certainly didn't start propagating lies. Those who say Jesus simply makes a false statement in Matthew 24:34 encounter another problem: if Jesus was wrong there, how can they believe anything else He said? At no time did Jesus ever say anything that wasn't true (Heb. 4:15). Thus it is unreasonable to believe that the phrase "this generation" refers to the disciples.

(*b*) The A.D. 70 theory

Many commentaries say that "this generation" refers to the disciples, and that the events of Matthew 24 were fulfilled at the destruction of Jerusalem in A.D. 70.

However, one must beware of confusing the destruction of Jerusalem in A.D. 70 with the second coming of Jesus Christ. At the beginning of Matthew 24, the disciples clearly asked Jesus what would be the sign of His coming. They didn't ask about when the Romans would come. And when Christ answered the disciples, He told them about the signs preceding His return.

Another problem with this view is that many of the events described in Matthew 24 didn't happen in A.D. 70. The sun and moon were not darkened; the stars didn't fall out of heaven (v. 29). Christ hasn't yet returned to gather the elect from the four corners of the earth (v. 31). There hasn't been mourning from all the tribes on the face of the earth (v. 30). The war in Jerusalem in A.D. 70 was between the Romans and the Jews—there weren't nations rising against nations (v. 7). There weren't earthquakes and pestilences all over the world on a scale never before known (v. 7).

Those who want to say the events of Matthew 24 took place in A.D. 70 say that Christ's teaching was only symbolic and that those events weren't supposed to happen literally. They say that Christ was only trying to emphasize the horrors of the destruction of Jerusalem. However, there is no good reason to believe that Jesus didn't mean exactly what He said.

(2) The Jewish race

Some people believe Jesus was referring to the Jewish race when He said "this generation." That's because the Greek word translated "generation" (*genea*) can be used to speak of a kind of people or a race. According to this view, Christ was saying, "The Jewish people will not die off until all these things come to pass." He would have been predicting the survival of the Jewish race until the second coming.

It's true that the Jewish people will survive until the second coming. But that's not a good interpretation of verse 34. If Jesus were talking about the Jewish race, it seems to me He would have said so. It would be off-handed for Him to refer to the covenant people as "this generation" when He could have said, "My people will not pass away until all these things be fulfilled." And, there was no question in the minds of the disciples that the Jewish people would survive until the second coming. They knew the Jewish people would survive because they trusted the lasting nature of God's covenants with them. That's not even an issue in the context.

(3) Those who reject Christ

Some people think Jesus was saying, "Those who reject and hate Me will be around until the second coming." The Greek word translated "generation" (*genea*) can be used in that way. In the Septuagint, the Greek version of the Old Testament, it is sometimes used to mean "this evil generation" and "this righteous generation." However, that interpretation is not consistent with the context of the passage or with what was uppermost in the minds of the disciples. They weren't concerned about whether evil people would survive up to the second coming or not; they were asking when the second coming would be and what signs would precede it.

(4) The nation of Israel

Many people believe the fig tree in Matthew 24:32 is Israel. They say the bursting forth of leaves represents the beginning of Israel's statehood in 1948. However, there's no way the disciples would have perceived His teaching that way. Remember that Jesus was teaching the parable to make things clear to them. For the new growth on the tree to refer to the establishment of the Jewish state in 1948 would be too obscure.

It's not logically consistent to conclude that the life pulsing through the fig tree refers to the statehood of Israel. That would be to say that there is new life in Israel. The nation was already alive physically, so the new life would have to be spiritual. But Israel is a secular nation today, so we can't say the new life represents a spiritual revival.

b) Who the generation is

The view most compatible with the context of the passage is that when a fig tree's branches are tender and it puts forth leaves, judgment is near. Those who see the signs in verses 4-28 should know that the Lord's return is near. The new leaves on the fig tree are analogous to the signs preceding the second coming. The phrase "this generation" clearly refers to the generation that is alive at the time those signs are fulfilled. Jesus was saying, "The generation that sees the signs of the second coming will not pass away until I return." That was Jesus' answer to the disciples' question of how much time would pass between the signs of His coming and His actual return. So once the birth pains begin (Matt. 24:8), everything else will happen in rapid succession.

Elsewhere Scripture specifies that the Tribulation will last for seven years (Dan. 9:27—each week in Daniel's seventy-week prophecy is seven years long). Its a time period known as Jacob's trouble (Jer. 30:7). In the book of Revelation we learn that the worst part of the Tribulation will be during the last three-and-a-half years (12:14), which is 1,260 days (11:3) or forty-two months (13:5). Jesus referred to that period as the Great Tribulation (Matt. 24:21). Its beginning will be marked by the abomination of desolation (Matt. 24:15-21).

2. The chronology

Who will be a part of the generation that is alive during the Tribulation and the second coming?

a) The post-Tribulation view

Some say the Christians alive before and during the Tribulation will be present at the second coming. They think the rapture will occur after the Tribulation—that we will meet the Lord in the air and then immediately return with Him to establish His kingdom.

b) The pre-Tribulation view

Others believe the church will be raptured before the Tribulation, spend those seven years with the Lord, and come back with Him when He returns to set up His kingdom. That's the view I hold.

Will the Church Go Through the Tribulation?

Let me explain why I believe those who are Christians now will not be a part of the generation that will be on earth when Christ returns.

1. The location of the church in the book of Revelation

The church is the theme of Revelation 2-3. The Lord expressed concern for the purity of the church and wrote to seven churches in Asia Minor. He ended chapter 3 by saying that He stands at the door and knocks. His second coming is inevitable, and He wants people to be ready for it.

In Revelation 4-5, we read that the church is in heaven. Then in chapter 6, the Tribulation begins. Chapters 6-18 detail the whole story of the Tribulation, but not once do we read about the church's being on earth or what it should do during the Tribulation. The absence of the church in Revelation 6-18 is significant, especially when you consider it is on earth in chapters 2-3 and then is in heaven in chapters 4-5.

2. The lack of instruction regarding the Tribulation

Nowhere in the New Testament are there any instructions about how the church is to endure the Tribulation. Nor is it mentioned when Christ taught about the Tribulation in Matthew 24. When I refer to the church, I mean those who are Christians from the time of Pentecost to the rapture. There will be Christians alive during the Tribulation, but they will be people who are saved after the Tribulation begins. Anyone who is a Christian prior to the Tribulation will be raptured with the rest of the church. The only church that appears on earth during the Tribulation is the false church, the religious system known as Babylon, which will be destroyed by God (Rev. 17-18).

3. The futility of a post-Tribulational rapture

First Thessalonians 4:17 describes the rapture: "We who are alive and remain shall be caught up . . . to meet the Lord in the air." It would be pointless for the rapture to happen at the end of the Tribulation. Why would Christ have us meet Him in the air if He's already on His way down? Besides, Revelation 19:14 indicates we already will be accompanying Him.

4. The dilemma of who will populate the kingdom

When the Lord comes, the Bible says, He will destroy all the wicked (Rev. 19:20-21). If the post-Tribulation view is correct, the only people left will be those who are already glorified because all the believers will have just been raptured. But the Bible tells us children will be born during the Tribulation (Isa. 11:6-8; 65:20). Since those who are glorified won't have children, where will those children come from if the wicked are gone and everyone raptured at the end of the Tribulation is glorified? Those children have to come from somewhere. In fact, they will produce a group of people who will rebel against Christ at the end of the millennial kingdom (Rev. 20:7-9). This is not a problem if the church is raptured at the beginning of the Tribulation, for only those saints will be glorified, and those who become saved during the Tribulation won't be glorified beings in Christ's kingdom. They will be able to bear children and populate the kingdom.

5. The promise to spare Christians from future wrath

God addresses believers in Revelation 3:10, saying, "Because thou hast kept the word of my patience, I also will keep thee from the hour of temptation, which shall come upon all the world, to try them that dwell upon the earth." The phrase "keep from" (Gk., *tēreō ek*) can be translated "outside." God was saying that He will keep the saints outside of "the hour of temptation, which shall come upon all the world." I believe that's a promise to all Christians that they will be rescued from the Tribulation. The phrase *tēreō ek* literally means "a state of continued existence outside." Thus the church won't be raptured in the middle of the Tribulation, as some say. Nor will it be kept within the Tribulation. *Tēreō en* means to exist within, but Revelation 3:10 uses *tēreō ek*, meaning we will exist outside the hour of temptation.

6. Jesus' plan to take believers to His Father's place

In John 14:3 Jesus says, "If I go and prepare a place for you, I will come again, and receive you unto myself, that where I am, there ye may be also." Christ is preparing a place for us in glory, and He will come to take us there with Him. But if the rapture takes place at the end of the Tribulation, we won't be able to go to that place to be with Christ. We would meet the Lord in the air, and return to the earth with Him immediately. However, Christ said He wants us to be where He is, and that's where we will go when we are raptured before the Tribulation. We will stay there until we return with Him to set up the glorious kingdom on earth.

7. The distinction in the purpose of the church and Israel

In Jeremiah 30:7 the Tribulation is known as "the time of Jacob's trouble." That's when God will go back to dealing with Israel. In Romans 11:17-24 we read that Israel is like a branch broken off from a tree, and that God grafted the church in its place. But there will come a time when the church is cut off and Israel is grafted back in (vv. 23-24). God isn't working through the nation of Israel today, but there is coming a time when He will deal with her again. In the seventy-week prophecy of Daniel 9, the church doesn't appear in the first sixty-nine weeks, and there is no reason for it to be around in the seventieth week (the Tribulation).

8. The concern of the Thessalonians

The Thessalonian church was sad because they thought those who had died would miss the rapture. Paul corrected that mistaken notion by saying, "I would not have you to be ignorant, brethren, concerning them who are asleep, that ye sorrow not, even as others who have no hope. . . . For this we say unto you by the word of the Lord, that we who are alive and remain unto the coming of the Lord shall not precede them who are asleep. . . . The dead in Christ shall rise first" (1 Thess. 4:13, 15-16). That the Thessalonians were sad shows they expected to be raptured before the Tribulation. Had they thought the rapture was *after* the Tribulation, they would have been happy for their dead brethren, thinking, *Those who are dead are lucky. We have to go through the Tribulation.* The Thessalonians were expecting to be with Christ in glory. They weren't expecting to have to endure the Tribulation and the Antichrist. That's consistent with the hope we all have as Christians—we await the glorious appearing of our Lord Jesus Christ (Titus 2:13).

Differences Between the Rapture and the Second Coming

At the rapture, the church will meet Christ in the air (1 Thess. 4:17). At the second coming, Christ will return to the earth with the church (Rev. 19:1). At the rapture, the Mount of Olives will remain intact; at the second coming, it will be split open (Zech. 14:4). At the rapture, believers will be transformed (1 Cor. 15:52); at the second coming, no one will be transformed. At the rapture, the world will not be judged. Instead, sin will become worse as the Tribulation progresses. At the second coming, sin will be judged and the world will become better (Rev. 19:17-21). The rapture could happen at any moment; the second coming will be preceded by some definite signs. The rapture concerns only the saved; the second coming concerns the saved and the unsaved. Thus the two events are distinct and are separated by a definite time period.

The phrase "this generation" in Matthew 24:34 refers to those who are left on the earth after the rapture because they weren't Christians. During the Tribulation 144,000 Jewish evangelists will witness for God all over the world (Rev. 7:4). They will bring many Jews and Gentiles to Christ. In fact, Revelation 7:9 says that so many Gentiles will be saved, they can't be counted. Those who become saved after the rapture and those who remain unsaved throughout the Tribulation will witness the signs of Christ's coming. They will be the generation that does not die off until all the events of Matthew 24 come to pass.

III. AN UNCHANGING AUTHORITY (v. 35)

"Heaven and earth shall pass away, but my words shall not pass away."

In Luke 16:17 Jesus says, "It is easier for heaven and earth to pass, than one tittle of the law to fail." In Matthew 5:18 He says, "Till heaven and earth pass, one jot or one tittle shall in no way pass from the law, till all be fulfilled." John 10:35 says, "The scripture cannot be broken." All that the Word of God says will happen will indeed come to pass.

Are you ready for the events of the future? Will you be raptured with the Lord's people and go into His presence, or will you be left to endure the holocaust that follows? If you aren't a believer, you aren't ready for Christ's return. If you are a Christian, Peter has these important words for you: "Seeing, then, that all these things shall be dissolved, what manner of persons ought ye to be in all holy living and godliness" (2 Pet. 3:11). We are to be looking for the coming of the Lord Jesus Christ and growing in grace.

Focusing on the Facts

1. What is the hope of every Christian? Support your answer with Scripture (see p. 102).
2. Explain the purpose of Jesus' parables (see pp. 102-3).
3. When fig trees start sprouting new leaves, that's a sign the harvest is near. What does Christ use harvests to illustrate in the New Testament (see p. 104)?
4. What was Jesus talking about when He said, "When ye shall see all these things" (Matt. 24:33; see p. 106)?
5. In the phrase "know that it is near," what does *it* refer to (Matt. 24:33; see p. 106)?
6. How do we know the disciples aren't the ones Jesus was referring to in Matthew 24:34 (see p. 107)?
7. What are the problems with saying that "this generation" refers to the Jewish race or to those who reject Christ (see p. 109)?
8. To whom does the phrase "this generation" refer (see p. 110)?
9. Define the post-Tribulation and pre-Tribulation views of the rapture (see p. 111).
10. What evidence in the book of Revelation gives support to the pre-Tribulation view of the rapture (see pp. 111-12)?
11. Scripture says there will be children in the millennial kingdom. What view of the rapture makes that possible, and why (see pp. 112-13)?
12. How might the Thessalonians have reacted to the death of their brothers and sisters in Christ if they thought the rapture was after the Tribulation (see p. 114)?
13. In what ways are the rapture and the second coming distinct from one another (see p. 114)?
14. What is Christ communicating in Matthew 24:35 (see p. 115)?

Pondering the Principles

1. Read Matthew 9:36-38. How did Jesus respond when He saw the multitudes? Why did He respond that way (v. 36)? What command did He give to the disciples in verse 38? Do you express the same feeling toward the lost that Jesus did? It's easy for some Christians to keep their distance from unsaved people because they're unsure of how much interaction they should have with unbelievers. Read Matthew 9:10-13. Why did Jesus

interact with sinners? His words in Matthew 9:37, "The harvest truly is plenteous, but the laborers are few," should motivate us to have compassion toward the lost. Seek every opportunity to bring unbelievers to Christ. Start by opening lines of communication with them.

2. In Matthew 24:35 Jesus says, "Heaven and earth shall pass away, but my words shall not pass away." God's Word will outlive the universe. Read Psalm 19:7-11, and meditate on the great truths about God's Word in that passage. How do those truths affect you?

3. Read 2 Peter 3:10-12. Those verses remind us that only things of a spiritual nature are lasting. The world as we know it will someday be destroyed. Memorize 2 Peter 3:11, and let it be a reminder to you of the priorities and focus you should have in all that you do: "Since all these things are to be destroyed in this way, what sort of people ought you to be in holy conduct and godliness" (NASB)?

8
Ready or Not, Here I Come!—Part 1

Outline

Introduction

Lesson
I. Pinpointing the Lord's Return (v. 36)
   A. The Exactness of the Time
   B. The Explanation About the Time
      1. It is not known by men
      2. It is not known by angels
      3. It is not known by the Son
         a) The comment
         b) The clarification
      4. It is known by the Father
   C. The Expectation of the Time
II. Preparing for the Lord's Return (vv. 37-51)
   A. Alertness (vv. 37-42)
      1. The prediction (v. 37)
         a) The extent of man's denial
            (1) As seen in the future
            (2) As seen in the past
         b) The extent of man's decadence
            (1) As seen in the future
            (2) As seen in the past
      2. The parallel (vv. 38-39)
         a) Noah's preaching
         b) The people's response
      3. The purging (vv. 40-41)
         a) The specifics
         b) The separation
      4. The preparation (v. 42)

Introduction

When I was a child, my friends and I played hide and seek. Someone was chosen to close his eyes and count for a while until everyone else had a chance to hide. When the person was finished counting, he would open his eyes and say, "Ready or not, here I come!"

That statement can be applied to the text of Matthew 24:36-51, which deals with the second coming of Jesus Christ. There we read of the suddenness and unexpectedness of His return. In this lesson we'll be examining verses 36-42, and we'll study the rest in the next lesson.

Lesson

I. PINPOINTING THE LORD'S RETURN (v. 36)

"Of that day and hour knoweth no man, no, not the angels of heaven, but my Father only."

Jesus told the disciples that the exact time of His return is unknown. The signs that precede His second coming have been clearly given throughout Matthew 24. Other signs that precede His return are mentioned in Revelation 6-18. The generation that is alive during the Tribulation will see those signs (Matt. 24:34). People all around the world will witness those signs; they will be obvious. However the specific moment of Christ's return—the exact day and hour—is not known.

A. The Exactness of the Time

Verses 13, 42, 44, and 50 all indicate that the exact moment of the Lord's return is unknown. The general time frame of the second coming will become obvious once people see all the signs in Matthew 24. The abomination of desolation will be a historical event. The wars, famines, pestilences, devastation, waters turning to blood, and increased darkness will all be noticed. But the exact day and hour of Christ's return won't be known; it will come unexpectedly.

120

All we know is that the coming of the Son of Man is "immediately after the tribulation" (vv. 29-30).

Both Daniel and Revelation tell us that the Great Tribulation—the second half of the Tribulation—will be three-and-a-half years long, forty-two months, or 1260 days (Dan. 7:25; 9:27; 12:7; Rev. 12:14; 13:5). The second half begins with the abomination of desolation in Matthew 24:15. That's when the Antichrist will demand to be worshiped. Matthew 24:29-30 says that immediately after that period the Son of Man will come. However, we don't know exactly how long it will be before the kingdom is actually established. In Daniel 12:11-12 we read about a seventy-five day period following the Tribulation, during which the kingdom will be established (see pp. 70-71).

The Tribulation will begin once the church is raptured. There will be three-and-a-half years of peace as the Antichrist politically rescues Israel and starts to revive what once composed the Roman Empire. Then in the middle of the seven-year Tribulation, he will desecrate the Temple in Jerusalem and demand that he be worshiped. The next three-and-a-half years will culminate in the return of Christ.

None of those things have happened yet. We don't know what generation they will come upon. It could be this generation; the church might be raptured any moment. And even those who do see the signs in Matthew 24 come to pass won't know the exact moment of Christ's return at the end of the Tribulation. That is a secret.

B. The Explanation About the Time

1. It is not known by men

Jesus specifically states in Matthew 24:36 that no man knows the day and hour of His coming. If men did know the exact moment of Christ's return, they would probably choose to live in sin until just before that moment. Christians might stop everything they are doing just to await the Lord's coming. Life would change considerably if you knew exactly when the Lord was going to come. People wouldn't make plans for the future; long-term relationships would be affected. So the Lord, in all His wisdom, has kept secret the time of Christ's return. He doesn't want people to take advantage of such knowledge for their own selfish reasons.

2. It is not known by angels

Matthew 24:36 also says that the angels of heaven don't know the day and hour of Christ's return. The natural world (mankind) doesn't know and neither does the supernatural world (the angels). The angels have constant access to God. In Isaiah 6 they hover around His throne awaiting His commands. In Matthew 18:10 we read they are face-to-face with God in intimate communion with Him. According to Matthew 13, angels will be the agents of judgment at the second coming. They are the reapers who will gather the wheat and tares and will throw the tares into a furnace of fire (vv. 37-42). Matthew 24:31 indicates that the angels will gather the believers who survive the Tribulation. Yet in spite of all those things, the angels still do not know the exact moment of Christ's coming. God has chosen not to reveal it to them. Scripture doesn't tell us why.

3. It is not known by the Son

   a) The comment

   The better manuscripts of Matthew indicate that Matthew 24:36 should read, "Of that day and hour knoweth no man, no, not the angels of heaven, *neither the Son*" (emphasis added). Mark 13:32, which is a parallel passage, includes that phrase.

   b) The clarification

   That Christ didn't know the time of His own return has created much discussion. How could Jesus Christ, who is God, not know something? Since He is God, isn't He omniscient? That's easily explained if we understand some facts about the incarnation. Jesus Christ is fully God (John 1:1, 14), but when He became a man, He voluntarily restricted the use of His divine attributes (Phil. 2:6-8). He didn't put His deity or divine attributes aside; He simply restricted the use of them. He lived without using His omniscience unless the Father prescribed for Him to use it.

Christ's omniscience is obvious in some passages. In John 2:24-25 we read that He knows what's in the heart of every man. In John 3 Jesus answers a question that Nicodemus had in mind but hadn't yet asked (vv. 1-3). In His incarnation, Christ restricted the use of His omniscience to those things that the Father wanted Him to know. Philippians 2:7 says He took upon Himself the form of a servant. He submitted Himself to whatever the Father wanted Him to do, say, or know. In John 15:15 Jesus says to the disciples, "Henceforth I call you not servants; for the servant knoweth not what his lord doeth: but I have called you friends; for all things that I have heard of my Father I have made known unto you." That verse explicitly states Jesus' knowledge was qualified by what the Father revealed to Him. Some of what He knew came through the Old Testament, some came from personal experiences during which He saw God's power, and some through direct revelation.

Jesus didn't have to restrict the use of His omniscience. But He chose to act as a servant to redeem mankind. That Jesus humbled Himself and took upon Himself the form of a servant means He limited the use of His divine attributes, including His omniscience. Scripture says that as Jesus grew older He "increased in wisdom and stature, and in favor with God and man" (Luke 2:52).

I believe after Christ was resurrected, the day and hour of His return became known to Him. After He came out of the grave in His resurrection glory, He said this to the disciples: "All authority is given unto me in heaven and in earth" (Matt. 28:18). Shortly afterwards He said, "It is not for you to know the times or the seasons [of the second coming], which the Father hath put in his own power" (Acts 1:7). He said only that the disciples wouldn't know the time of His return; He didn't include Himself as He did in Matthew 24:36 and Mark 13:32. So when Christ rose from the dead, He resumed full use of His attributes and therefore had full knowledge of when His second coming would be.

4. It is known by the Father

   At the end of Matthew 24:36 Jesus says only the Father knows the time of the second coming. (Jesus always called the first member of the Godhead "Father" with only one exception: in Matthew 27:46 He said, "My God, my God, why hast thou forsaken me?" because He was temporarily separated from the Father as He was bearing all the sins of the world on the cross.) The word *only* is significant. Only the Father knew the time of the second coming when Jesus made that statement. Yet as we discussed, now that Christ is risen, He knows too.

C. The Expectation of the Time

   God doesn't want mankind to know when the second coming will be because He wants every generation to live in expectation of it. He wants everyone to be prepared at all times. So ever since the New Testament era, Christians have always lived in eager anticipation of the second coming.

   1. 1 Corinthians 1:6-7—"The testimony of Christ was confirmed in you; so that ye come behind in no gift, waiting for the coming of our Lord Jesus Christ." The first generation church in Corinth anticipated Christ's return.

   2. Hebrews 10:24-25—"Let us consider one another to provoke unto love and to good works, not forsaking the assembling of ourselves together, as the manner of some is, but exhorting one another, and so much the more, as ye see the day approaching." That was written as if those who received the letter of Hebrews would witness Christ's return.

   3. Philippians 3:20—"Our citizenship is in heaven, from which also we look for the Savior, the Lord Jesus Christ." We look to heaven in anticipation of Christ's coming.

4. James 5:8—"Be ye also patient, establish your hearts; for the coming of the Lord draweth near."

5. 1 Peter 4:7—"The end of all things is at hand; be ye, therefore, soberminded, and watch unto prayer."

6. 1 John 2:18—"Little children, it is the last time."

7. Revelation 22:20—"He who testifieth these things [Jesus] saith, Surely, I come quickly. Amen. Even so, come, Lord Jesus."

The writers of the New Testament didn't fully understand how much time would go by before the second coming of Christ, but they lived in expectation of it. Every generation should be prepared for His return. If we knew when Christ planned to return, then no one would live in expectation until just before the right moment.

Why Is Christ Waiting So Long Before He Returns?

1. He is permitting evil to run its course

Revelation 14:15-16 says, "Another angel came out of the temple, crying with a loud voice to him that sat on the cloud, Thrust in thy sickle, and reap; for the time is come for thee to reap; for the harvest of the earth is ripe. And he that sat on the cloud thrust in his sickle on the earth, and the earth was reaped." The imagery there is important: only when grain is ripe is it harvested. And the Lord is waiting for the ripening of evil. God will not enact judgment on this world until the harvest is ripe—until sin has run its course. He will wait until all evil has been revealed. It's hard to imagine that things could get any worse in our world, but that's what God is waiting for before He takes the sickle and executes His judgment.

2. He is adding to His church

Paul writes in Romans 11:25, "I would not, brethren, that ye should be ignorant of this mystery, lest ye should be wise in your own conceits: that blindness in part is happened to Israel, until the fullness of the Gentiles be come in." The phrase "the fullness of the Gentiles" refers to the gathering in of the church in this age. After the fullness of the time of the Gentiles (the church age), the Lord will then allow many Jewish people to become saved (Rom. 11:26) during the Tribulation.

3. He is not bound by time

Second Peter 3:8 says, "Beloved, be not ignorant of this one thing, that one day is with the Lord as a thousand years, and a thousand years as one day." God doesn't keep a clock, yet we are creatures of time. Thus what seems like a long time for us is no time at all to the eternal God. Verse 9 continues, "The Lord is not slack concerning his promise, as some men count slackness, but is longsuffering toward us, not willing that any should perish, but that all should come to repentance." God is waiting until all the Gentiles and Jewish people destined to become saved are redeemed. Then Christ will return.

a) The precedence

Backing up to verses 3-4 we read, "Knowing this first, that there shall come in the last days scoffers, walking after their own lusts, and saying, Where is the promise of his coming? For since the fathers [i.e., the patriarchs] fell asleep, all things continue as they were from the beginning of the creation." There are people who deny Christ will come. They say everything will continue as usual; nothing will ever change. But verses 5-6 say, "They willingly are ignorant of, that by the word of God the heavens were of old, and the earth standing out of the water and in the water, by which the world that then was, being overflowed with water, perished."

Those who say nothing has ever changed overlook the Flood. God wiped out the entire world—except for eight people—in the Flood (Gen. 7-8). There is physical evidence all over the globe to support that. Why did the Flood come? Because God "saw that the wickedness of man was great in the earth" (Gen. 6:5). All things will not continue as they have. There is coming a time of judgment.

b) The prophecy

Second Peter 3:10 says, "The day of the Lord will come as a thief in the night." It will come suddenly and unexpectedly.

Then we read that "the heavens shall pass away with a great noise, and the elements shall melt with fervent heat; the earth also, and the works that are in it, shall be burned up." When the Lord returns to set up the millennial kingdom, the heavens and the earth will be dramatically changed. As Matthew 24 says, the stars will fall, and the moon and sun won't give light (v. 29). The waters and the terrain of the earth will be changed (Rev. 6:14; 8:8-9). There will be much chaos as the heavens and the earth are changed at the onset of the millennium. Then at the end of the millennial kingdom there will come a *new* heaven and earth (Rev. 21:1). Thus the changes in the heavens and the earth will occur in two phases: first there will be a modification of the universe when Jesus comes. Then there will be a completely new and eternal heaven and earth created at the end of the thousand-year kingdom.

The Lord created a perfect world, and then it fell into sin. The world will be restored in some way at the beginning of Christ's earthly reign, but ultimately the heavens and the earth will be completely re-created in eternity. We see the history of the universe in 2 Peter 3.

II. PREPARING FOR THE LORD'S RETURN (vv. 37-51)

Since no one knows the exact time of Christ's return, how should each generation respond, especially those who see the birth pains—the disasters, the changes on the face of the earth, and the abomination of desolation? We will examine three attitudes: alertness, readiness, and faithfulness. The last two we will look at in the next lesson.

A. Alertness (vv. 37-42)

1. The prediction (v. 37)

"As the days of Noah were, so shall also the coming of the Son of man be."

The Flood is the only event in human history that comes close to illustrating what will happen in the end times, for the Flood destroyed everything on earth. The attitude that prevailed during the time of Noah will be the attitude that prevails before the second coming.

When Noah told the people that God's judgment was near, they didn't care. Similarly, people during the end times will notice all the signs and wonders going on around them, but many of them won't consider what's happening and why.

a) The extent of man's denial

   (1) As seen in the future

   Second Peter 3:3 says, "There shall come in the last days scoffers." People will be using their computers and charts in an attempt to analyze the universe and explain scientifically why everything is going haywire. They will try to explain away the earthquakes and abnormal tide activity. They will try to figure out why there are abnormal changes in the heavens—why the sun and moon aren't working as they usually do. People will attempt to rationalize why the seas are bitter and why people are being massacred on an unprecedented scale. In so doing, they will completely overlook the truth in God's Word.

   Men will be no different at the Lord's second coming than they were at His first coming. Many people saw Jesus, heard Him, and watched Him banish disease from the land of Palestine. They saw Him raise the dead. Yet they still didn't receive Him as Lord. In fact, the Jewish religious leaders concluded He was of the devil (Matt. 12:24). The people who lived at the time Christ was on earth were selfish, sinful, and so devoid of spiritual perception that they didn't even recognize the Savior when He walked in their midst. Things won't be any different when people see the signs preceding Christ's coming again.

(2) As seen in the past

In the beginning of Matthew 16, the Pharisees and Sadducees came to Jesus and asked Him to "show them a sign from heaven" (v. 1). They wanted Him to prove He was the Messiah, but they had already seen many signs by this time. Jesus answered, "When it is evening, ye say, It will be fair weather; for the sky is red. And in the morning, It will be foul weather today; for the sky is red and overcast. O ye hypocrites, ye can discern the face of the sky, but can ye not discern the signs of the times?" (vv. 2-3). They were great at figuring out the weather, but they didn't have a clue as to what God was doing in their midst.

The religious leaders had shut their minds to the truth of God. Throughout Israel's history they had ignored the miracles and warnings of God's prophets, going to the extent of murdering them. They eventually even murdered the Son of God. When the signs preceding Christ's return come to pass, the world will be just as blind as the Jewish leaders were. People will not perceive what is happening. They will try to explain everything away.

b) The extent of man's decadence

(1) As seen in the future

Second Thessalonians 2:6-8 tells us that during the Tribulation the Holy Spirit will remove His restraining effect on evil. Right now the Spirit is holding back the evil of the world, but it seems that as time goes on, He's slowly pulling back the restraints. And when the Tribulation comes, evil will be allowed to run its full course. Demons that are temporarily bound will overrun the earth (Rev. 9:1-3). The archangel Michael will fight with Satan, and Satan will be cast out of heaven to earth (Rev. 12:7-9). So with Satan and his demons running loose, sin will become rampant. The phrase "mystery of iniquity" is used in 2 Thessalonians 2:7 to describe the extent of the evil of that time. It will be worse than any other time in history. The world will be preoccupied more than ever with sin, illicit sex, drugs, alcohol, and materialism. People will hate God, each other, and the truth.

(2) As seen in the past

During the Tribulation, the world will be as it was in the days of Noah. According to 2 Peter 2:5, Noah was "a preacher of righteousness." He built a large ark in the middle of the desert and told people there would be a flood. They laughed at him because it had never rained on the earth up to that time. He spent 120 years building the ark (Gen. 6:3) and was probably asked the same question over and over, "Why are you building that?" Noah most likely answered, "Because God is going to judge the wicked of this world and only those who put their faith in Him are going to escape. Would you like to join me?" For 120 years people went on with life as usual and ignored Noah's preaching. However, Noah didn't let that discourage him; he continued building the ark, which was about the size of a modern ocean liner. The scoffers didn't want to hear about God's judgment; they probably came up with all kinds of reasons not to believe Noah.

2. The parallel (vv. 38-39)

"In the days that were before the flood they were eating and drinking, marrying and giving in marriage, until the day that Noah entered into the ark, and knew not until the flood came, and took them all away, so shall also the coming of the Son of man be."

a) Noah's preaching

Noah preached for 120 years, and those who heard him didn't believe him until they saw the heavy rains that started the Flood. During the Great Tribulation there will be many signs warning of Christ's coming.

There will be many preachers of righteousness in that time: the 144,000 Jewish evangelists and the multitude of Gentiles of Revelation 7, and the two witnesses sent from God of Revelation 11. There will also be an angel who preaches the gospel message to all the people on the earth (Rev. 14:6). But many people will not believe what they hear until it's too late. They will come up with all kinds of reasons to scoff and laugh. If people were that wicked in the days of Noah, you can imagine how much worse they will be in the last days before Christ's coming.

b) The people's response

Matthew 24:38 says that before the Flood, people were "eating and drinking, marrying and giving in marriage." Eating and drinking aren't sins; neither is marriage. The problem was that life went on as usual. The people lived as if nothing would happen to them. They disregarded Noah's preaching. Social, family, and business life went on as usual. That's exactly what will happen during the Tribulation.

Sometimes when we envision the Tribulation, we think surely the terrible events in that time will cause people to recognize that the end of the world is coming. Some will recognize it; they will be the redeemed remnant. But in general there will be a massive, worldwide rejection of anything that is associated with God.

Everyone but Noah's family rejected God. And by the time God had shut the door of the ark and the rains began, it was too late for anyone to change his mind. Once the floodwaters started rising, I'm sure some people knocked on the door of the ark. But it was too late. Matthew 24:39 says they didn't realize what was happening "until the flood came." The Greek word translated "flood" is *kataklusmos*, from which we get the English word *cataclysm*. It means "to wash down." All the wicked people were washed away into damnation and judgment. Verse 39 continues, "So shall also the coming of the Son of man be."

The same thing will happen at the second coming. Life will go on as usual until it's too late.

The people in Noah's generation were warned for 120 years. The generation that lives through the Tribulation will be warned. In reality, we are all being warned now. Ever since the New Testament was written, it has warned every generation that Christ could come at any time. But most people won't heed the warning until they are swept away in judgment.

3. The purging (vv. 40-41)

"Then shall two be in the field; the one shall be taken, and the other left. Two women shall be grinding at the mill; the one shall be taken, and the other left."

a) The specifics

The Greek word translated "one" is masculine in verse 40 and feminine in verse 41. So verse 40 talks about two men in a field; verse 41 speaks of two women grinding at a mill. In Bible times, the men of Israel generally worked in the fields, and the women ground what was harvested by the men. Jesus was saying that in the routine of life, one will be taken and the other left when Christ returns.

b) The separation

Some people believe Jesus was referring to the rapture, but as we've seen already, the rapture will happen prior to the Tribulation. Since verses 40-41 follow right after what verse 39 said about people's being washed away in judgment, we know that Jesus was referring to judgment—only now in reference to the second coming. The people who are taken will be taken in judgment, and those who are left will inhabit Christ's kingdom. They are those who became saved during the Tribulation. So one day while people are working, the unbelievers will be taken in judgment, and the believers will be preserved.

The judgment process is described in greater detail in Matthew 25:31-46, where the sheep (believers) are separated from the goats. The sheep will remain to inhabit the eternal kingdom, but the goats will be sent into everlasting punishment. Thus when the millennial kingdom begins, there will be believers on earth who will inhabit it. They will be those who lived through the Antichrist's reign of terror. All the ungodly will be swept away in judgment.

Acts 2:19-21 says that in the midst of all the destruction during the Tribulation, anyone who calls "on the name of the Lord shall be saved" (v. 21). Even those who call upon the Lord just before judgment will be in the kingdom along with those who were believers during the Tribulation. They will be the ones who populate the earth and have children during the millennium (see pp. 112-13).

4. The preparation (v. 42)

"Watch, therefore; for ye know not what hour your Lord doth come."

No one will know the exact time of Christ's return. Even the generation alive during the Tribulation won't know. People will be going through life as usual, and suddenly some will be taken and others left. There is coming a day when the door to the kingdom will be shut forever. The parable of the virgins (Matt. 25:1-13) confirms that.

Who Will Be Spared from the Wrath to Come?

The Lord knows whom He will leave and whom He will take. Malachi 3:16-17 says, "They that feared the Lord spoke often one to another; and the Lord hearkened, and heard it, and a book of remembrance was written before him for them that feared the Lord, and that thought upon his name. And they shall be mine, saith the Lord of hosts, in that day when I make up my jewels; and I will spare them, as a man spareth his own son that serveth him." God knows who belongs to Him.

In 2 Peter 2 we read, "If God spared not the angels that sinned, but cast them down to hell, and delivered them into chains of darkness, to be reserved unto judgment; and spared not the old world, but saved Noah, the eighth person, a preacher of righteousness, bringing in the flood upon the world of the ungodly; and, turning the cities of Sodom and Gomorrah into ashes, condemned them with an overthrow, making them an example unto those that after should live ungodly, and delivered just Lot . . . the Lord knoweth how to deliver the godly out of temptations, and to reserve the unjust unto the day of judgment to be punished" (vv. 4-7, 9). Since God knew how to get Lot out of Sodom and Gomorrah, Noah out of the Flood, and the holy angels out of the devastation of heaven, He will surely know how to sort out the righteous and unrighteous in the judgment to come.

The second coming of Christ is not fantasy—it is fact. Just as the first coming of Christ was prophesied and fulfilled, so the second coming. If Christ is not your Lord now, He will become your Lord in eternity by exercising His right to send you into eternal punishment. Philippians 2:10 says there is coming a day when "at the name of Jesus every knee should bow." Some will bow in adoration; others will bow in terror. Willingly or unwillingly, every person will profess that Christ is Lord.

Focusing on the Facts

1. What do we know about the moment that Christ will return to earth? Support your answer with Scripture (see pp. 120-21).
2. What did Jesus say regarding the knowledge of when He will return? Be specific (Matt. 24:36; see p. 121).
3. What confusion arises with the phrase "neither the Son" in Matthew 24:36? What explanation can be given to eliminate that confusion (see pp. 122-24)?
4. Why doesn't God want mankind to know when Christ will return (see p. 124)?
5. What Scripture verses verify the early church's anticipation of the second coming (see pp. 124-25)?
6. What are some reasons that Christ is waiting before He returns to earth (see pp. 125-27)?
7. What prediction is made in Matthew 24:37 (see pp. 127-28)?

8. How will most people respond to the events of the Tribulation (see p. 128)?
9. According to 2 Thessalonians 2:6-8, what will happen during the Tribulation (see pp. 129-30)?
10. While Noah built the ark, he warned people of God's coming judgment. How did they respond (Matt. 24:38-39; see p. 131)?
11. What was Jesus talking about when He said, "One shall be taken, and the other left" (Matt. 24:40-41; see p. 132)?
12. What exhortation does Christ conclude with in Matthew 24:42 (see p. 133)?

Pondering the Principles

1. Completely understanding how Christ's human nature and divine nature worked together is impossible. Yet the Bible confirms that Jesus was indeed God incarnate. Through the ages people have said that Christ couldn't be God because He didn't know the time of His second coming (Mark 13:32). Read the following verses: Matthew 17:27; John 1:47-48, 2:25; and John 13:38 with 18:27. What do those verses confirm about Christ's knowledge? What are some other affirmations of Christ's deity that you can think of from Scripture? Here's a good way to see Christ's deity on display: Each day this week, read three chapters from the book of John. As you read, keep a record of all the passages you find that affirm Christ's deity. Share what you learn with others.

2. It's sobering to read Scripture passages that warn of God's future judgment upon the world. Such passages help us to have greater compassion for unbelievers. The apostle Paul suggests one action you can take in response: "I urge that entreaties and prayers, petitions and thanksgivings, be made on behalf of all men" (1 Tim. 2:1, NASB). God wants us to cultivate a habit of praying consistently for *all* men. You can start now by praying regularly for unsaved relatives, friends, and coworkers.

9
Ready or Not, Here I Come!—Part 2

Outline

Introduction

Review
I. Pinpointing the Lord's Return (v. 36)
II. Preparing for the Lord's Return (vv. 37-51)
  A. Alertness (vv. 37-42)

Lesson
  B. Readiness (vv. 43-44)
    1. The unknown element (v. 43)
    2. The unquestionable exhortation (v. 44)
  C. Faithfulness (vv. 45-51)
    1. The criteria (vv. 45-47)
      a) The responsibility to be obedient (v. 45)
      b) The reward for being obedient (v. 46)
      c) The result of being obedient (v. 47)
    2. The condemnation (vv. 48-51)
      a) Fatal procrastination
      b) False piety

Conclusion

Introduction

Every Christian lives in anticipation of Christ's second coming. Theologian Oscar Cullmann said that the Christian exists in a tension between what is and is to be (*Salvation in History* [New York: Harper & Row, 1967], p. 172). Believers have already experienced salvation, but they have not experienced the fullness of salvation—the redemption of their bodies (Rom. 8:23). They have already received the power of the Holy Spirit, but they haven't yet seen the fullness of that power, which they will experience in heaven. They have already received eternal life but haven't participated in the resurrection of the dead. Thus believers live in tension. They look back to the cross and look forward to the second coming. They live near the last days but don't live in the last days. They look at what God as already done and await what has not yet come to pass.

The writer of Hebrews portrayed the believer's anticipation of the second coming this way: "So Christ was once offered to bear the sins of many; and unto them that look for him shall he appear the second time without sin unto salvation" (Heb. 9:28). Peter wrote, "Blessed be the God and Father of our Lord Jesus Christ, who, according to his abundant mercy, hath begotten us again unto a living hope by the resurrection of Jesus Christ from the dead, to an inheritance incorruptible, and undefiled, and that fadeth not away, reserved in heaven for you" (1 Pet. 1:3-4). Believers have been born again but haven't entered fully into their inheritance. First John 3:2 says, "It doth not yet appear what we shall be, but we know that, when he shall appear, we shall be like him; for we shall see him as he is." They have received Christ but aren't completely like Him yet.

Thus Christians live between what is and is to be. Their hearts are filled with anticipation of Christ's return. But that's not true for those who don't know Christ. Anyone who hears about Christ's second coming but isn't ready for it should live in fear. Paul wrote, "Knowing, therefore, the terror of the Lord, we persuade men" (2 Cor. 5:11). Hebrews 10:31 says, "It is a fearful thing to fall into the hands of the living God." For some, the second coming of Christ brings thoughts of hope and future glory, but for others it brings fear and dread of eternal doom. Those who know the Savior love His appearing, but unbelievers fear His appearing.

I. PINPOINTING THE LORD'S RETURN (v. 36; see pp. 120-27)

II. PREPARING FOR THE LORD'S RETURN (vv. 37-51)

In Matthew 24:36 Jesus warns that the exact time of His return is unknown. In verses 37-51 He tells us three attitudes we should have with respect to His return.

A. Alertness (vv. 37-42; see pp. 127-34)

Lesson

B. Readiness (vv. 43-44)

1. The unknown element (v. 43)

"But know this, that if the householder had known in what watch the thief would come, he would have watched, and would not have allowed his house to be broken into."

The phrase "but know this" is in contrast to what Jesus says in verse 42: "Ye know not what hour your Lord doth come." The phrase "that if" shows Jesus is talking about something contrary to fact. The term "watch" refers to one of four three-hour periods during the night. The Jews divided the night into time periods from 6:00 to 9:00 P.M., 9:00 P.M. to 12:00 midnight, 12:00 midnight to 3:00 A.M., and 3:00 to 6:00 A.M. "Broken into" is translated from a Greek word that means "to dig through." In those days, thieves broke into homes by digging through mud walls or tile roofs.

The Lord was saying this: if a man knew when a thief was coming—not the exact minute or hour but the general time—then he would be ready. In the New Testament, Christ's second coming is often likened to the coming of a thief (Luke 12:35-40; 1 Thess. 5:2; 2 Pet. 3:10; Rev. 3:3; 16:15). That's not because Christ is like a thief;

it's because He will come suddenly and unexpectedly. And when a thief breaks into a home, he generally takes many things. That's what will happen when Christ returns. He will burn everything that cannot stand the test of judgment.

The Lord is coming unexpectedly. He will come suddenly at a time when no one will be watching for Him. It's hard to imagine that because you would think that after the rapture, people would anticipate Christ's return. But sin blinds people. "The mystery of iniquity" (2 Thess. 2:7) will reach its apex in the end times. People will try to explain away the signs preceding Christ's coming. They will become hostile toward God. Some people who initially said, "Christ will come soon," will eventually change their minds and say, "He isn't coming." It's possible that once the signs of Matthew 24 are over with, things will settle into some modicum of normality long enough for people to think nothing else will happen. And that's when Christ will come—when people least expect Him. However it happens, people won't be ready for the moment.

2. The unquestionable exhortation (v. 44)

"Therefore be ye also ready; for in such an hour as ye think not the Son of man cometh."

Some people will watch all the signs preceding Christ's return and then try to receive Christ at the last possible moment. But the Lord won't allow for that. He said, "You don't know when I'm coming, and I'm not coming when you think I am." Scripture doesn't tell us exactly how much time will occur after the Tribulation and before the sign of the Son of Man (Matt. 24:29-30). Somehow the world will be lulled into thinking that Christ won't come immediately. But that's when Christ will come in His final fury and glory.

The point of Jesus' analogy in Matthew 24:43-44 is simple. If a man knew a thief was coming, he'd be ready. And if you know Jesus is coming, you'd better be ready. Since we don't know when Christ will return, we need to be ready all the time.

The Reward for Those Who Are Ready

In Luke 12, Christ gives the same warning about His return in different terms. He said, "Let your loins be girded about, and your lamps burning; and ye yourselves like men that wait for their lord, when he will return from the wedding; that when he cometh and knocketh, they may open unto him immediately. Blessed are those servants, whom the lord, when he cometh, shall find watching; verily I say unto you, that he shall gird himself, and make them to sit down to eat, and will come forth and serve them" (vv. 35-37). When the Lord comes back, if you've been faithful, He will set you down to eat and serve you. The faithful Christian does not know when Christ is coming, but he's ready.

It's one thing to be alert and say, "I'll recognize the signs preceding Christ's coming." It's something else to be ready with a prepared heart by receiving Christ as your Savior. Let's look at the next element necessary for the Lord's coming.

C. Faithfulness (vv. 45-51)

1. The criteria (vv. 45-47)

   a) The responsibility to be obedient (v. 45)

   "Who, then, is a faithful and wise servant, whom his lord hath made ruler over his household, to give them food in due season?"

   Here Christ gives a parable. The lord represents God, and the servant represents every man and woman. We have all been given a great responsibility. It's as if the Lord said, "Manage everything I gave you in creating you in My image—your intellect, will, emotions, and talents—and all the other good things I have given you. Use them all for serving Me." We are like the servant who is told to manage all the goods in a house and to dispense food to everyone at the right time and place.

   Everything we have was granted to us by God. We are accountable for how we manage all those things.

Hell will be populated not only by the devil and his angels but also by those who wasted the privileges God gave them. And those who misuse what God has given them will be condemned, as was the man who embezzled the king's money in Matthew 18.

b) The reward for being obedient (v. 46)

"Blessed is that servant, whom his lord, when he cometh, shall find so doing."

When the Lord returns, He will bless the servants who are doing what He wanted them to do. Those who are obedient give evidence of being believers. Doing the will of God is always the mark of true salvation. True Christians will be found making the most of their stewardship.

c) The result of being obedient (v. 47)

"Verily I say unto you that he shall make him ruler over all his goods."

When the Lord returns, He will allow His faithful servants to manage everything He possesses. Have you ever wondered what we will be doing in the millennial kingdom and in eternity? We will sit with Christ on His throne and rule over everything He possesses (Rev. 3:21). So what a person does during his short life on earth will determine whether he will rule in eternity with Christ or be dominated by the demons in hell. The person who is proved faithful to God will be rewarded.

2. The condemnation (vv. 48-51)

"But and if that evil servant shall say in his heart, My lord delayeth his coming; and shall begin to smite his fellow servants, and to eat and drink with the drunkards, the lord of that servant shall come in a day when he looketh not for him, and in an hour that he is not aware of, and shall cut him asunder, and appoint him his portion with the hypocrites; there shall be weeping and gnashing of teeth."

When the Lord returns, He will unmask unfaithful stewards. They will be those whose oil lamps weren't trimmed (Matt. 25:7-8), who buried the talent entrusted to them instead of investing it (Matt. 25:18). They will be cast into outer darkness, where there is weeping and gnashing of teeth (Matt. 25:30).

a) Fatal procrastination

The word *evil* in the phrase "evil servant" speaks of those who are evil in nature. According to verse 48, such people will say, "My lord delayeth his coming." Even though they may observe the signs of Christ's coming, they will wait until the last possible moment to turn to Christ. Instead of using their resources for others, they will squander them on themselves. They will abuse others and live an indulgent life-style.

You may have heard people say, "I'll watch for the rapture. Once it happens, I know I'll still have a little while left to live in sin. I'll watch for the signs of Christ's return, the abomination of desolation, and all the events of Revelation 6-18. Then when I see the sign of the Son of Man in heaven, I'll start being careful because I don't know exactly what will happen after that. Then I'll repent of my sins. In the meantime, I can enjoy myself." But Matthew 24:50 warns, "The lord of that servant shall come in a day when he looketh not for him, and in an hour that he is not aware of." Don't try to slide into the kingdom at the last minute. If you won't give your heart to Christ now, what makes you think you will give it to Him in the future?

Some people say they will receive Christ when they feel ready. But if they don't want to receive Him now when sin is still being restrained by the Holy Spirit, why should they want to receive Christ when sin is completely unrestrained? The world will become worse than it has ever been. Those who enjoy gratifying their lusts now will want to gratify their lusts even more during the Tribulation. Anyone who wants to put off receiving Christ until just before His return will be unsuccessful in his attempt. Christ

Himself said clearly that no one knows the day or hour of His return. Many people may have waited until the floodwaters were up to their knees before they started banging on the door of Noah's ark. But by that time it was too late.

b) False piety

Not all unregenerate people live overtly sinful lives. Verse 51 says there are others who are hypocrites—people who pretend to be religious. Both those who live in sin to an excessive degree and those who are religious phonies will think Christ has delayed His coming—and both will ultimately end up in the same place. Hell is for all categories of unregenerate people.

Matthew 24:51 specifies the fate of those found to be unfaithful servants at Christ's return. The Lord will cut them asunder. The word translated "cut" (Gk., *dichotomeō*) means "to dichotomize." That word is used in the Septuagint in Exodus 29:17 to speak of cutting sacrificial animals in half. In Matthew 24:51 the Lord is illustrating the deadly seriousness of God's judgment. The person who tries to get away with doing whatever he wants and receiving Christ at the last possible moment will pay a severe price. He will be cut in half, spending the rest of eternity weeping and gnashing his teeth with other unbelievers. The book of Matthew mentions several times the weeping and gnashing of teeth that will go on in hell (8:12; 13:42, 50; 22:13; 25:30). That's a vivid description of the unrelieved torment of eternal hell.

Conclusion

How are we to be prepared for the unexpected and sudden coming of Christ? We are to be alert, ready, and faithful. We need to be watching for the signs, ready for His coming, and faithful to the Lord's Word and the stewardship He has given us. In 1 Thessalonians 5:2-3 Paul writes, "[You] yourselves know perfectly that the day of the Lord so cometh as a thief in the night. For when they shall say, Peace and safety, then sudden destruction cometh upon them, as travail upon a woman with child, and they shall not escape." At the Tribulation and prior to the Lord's return, people will say that peace is at hand and that all will return to normal. But that's when sudden destruction will come upon them, just as labor pains come upon a woman about to have a child. They will not escape. They will find themselves facing God and judgment.

Paul continues in verses 4-5, "Ye, brethren, are not in darkness, that that day should overtake you as a thief. Ye are all sons of light." The day of Christ's return will not take us by surprise because we won't go through the Tribulation. God "hath not appointed us to wrath, but to obtain salvation by our Lord Jesus Christ" (v. 9). We are children of the light, and God will remove us from the world before darkness falls. We don't have to worry about the Tribulation. But those who aren't ready before the rapture will go through the Tribulation. And if they still aren't ready at the end of the Tribulation, sudden destruction will come upon them when they least expect it. I hope you're ready for the Lord's return.

Only the Devils Say There's No Hurry

Commentator William Barclay relates this story illustrating the danger of procrastination:

"There is a fable which tells of three apprentice devils who were coming to this earth to finish their apprenticeship. They were talking to Satan, the chief of the devils, about their plans to tempt and ruin men. The first said, 'I will tell them there is no God.' Satan said, 'That will not delude many, for they know there is a God.' The second said, 'I will tell men there is no hell.' Satan answered, 'You will deceive no one that way; men know even now that there is a hell for sin.' The third said, 'I will tell men there is no hurry.' 'Go,' said Satan, 'and you will ruin them by the thousand'" (*The Gospel of Matthew*, vol. 2 [Philadelphia: Westminster, 1975], p. 317).

There *is* a hurry. Paul wrote, "Now it is high time to awake out of sleep; for now is our salvation nearer than when we believed. The night is far spent, the day is at hand; let us, therefore, cast off the works of darkness, and let us put on the armor of light" (Rom. 13:11-12). Each day, we move closer and closer to the second coming of Christ. Are you ready?

Focusing on the Facts

1. Describe the tension all Christians live in (see p. 137-38).
2. The reality of the second coming brings thoughts of what to those who are saved? To those who are not saved (see p. 138)?
3. In the New Testament, Christ's second coming is likened to the coming of a thief. Why is that (see pp. 139-40)?
4. For what are we accountable to God (see p. 141)?
5. What will happen to those who are good stewards of what God has given them (Matt. 24:46-47; see p. 142)?
6. What will happen to those who are found to be unfaithful servants (Matt. 24:51; see pp. 142-43)?
7. What are two characteristics that will mark the unsaved people of the end times (Matt. 24:48-51; see pp. 143-44)?
8. Some people say they will receive Christ when they feel ready. What is wrong with their logic, especially if they go on to live through the Tribulation (see p. 143)?
9. What did Paul say would happen someday at the end of the Tribulation and prior to the Lord's return (1 Thess. 5:2-3; see pp. 144-45)?
10. What exhortation does Paul give in Romans 13:11-12 (see p. 145)?

Pondering the Principles

1. Luke 12:35-36 says in regard to the second coming, "Let your loins be girded about, and your lamps burning; and ye yourselves like men that wait for their lord." That speaks of the necessity of being prepared at all times for Christ's return. On a scale of 1-10, how ready are you mentally? How ready are you spiritually? What can you do to be more prepared? Those are questions you'll want to ask yourself frequently in the future. That's because having an attitude of preparedness will have a positive, cleansing effect on your life-style.

2. Get together with another Christian and ask yourselves this question: *If I had only twenty-four hours left to live on this earth, how would I use them?* This activity will give insight into how you can become a better steward of your time and other resources God has given you.

10
The Fate of the Unprepared

Outline

Introduction
A. The Subject of the Parable
B. The Simplicity of the Parable

Lesson
I. The Wedding (v. 1)
   A. The Arrangement of a Marriage
     1. The engagement
     2. The betrothal
     3. The wedding
   B. The Anticipation Before a Marriage
II. The Bridesmaids (vv. 1-5)
   A. Their Supplies
   B. Their Status
     1. Socially
       a) The selection of virgin bridesmaids
       b) The significance of virgin bridesmaids
       c) The sum of virgin bridesmaids
     2. Spiritually
       a) The outward appearance
       b) The inward reality
   C. Their Slumber
     1. Christ's remark about a long wait
     2. Christian responsibility during the long wait
III. The Bridegroom (vv. 6-12)
   A. The Arrival
   B. The Awakening
   C. The Appeal
   D. The Answer

E. The Abandoning
    1. The reception into the kingdom
    2. The rejection from the kingdom
IV. The Warning (v. 13)

Conclusion

Introduction

Let's begin by reading Matthew 25:1-13, the Scripture passage we'll be examining in this lesson: "Then shall the kingdom of heaven be likened unto ten virgins, who took their lamps, and went forth to meet the bridegroom. And five of them were wise, and five were foolish. They that were foolish took their lamps, and took no oil with them; but the wise took oil in their vessels with their lamps. While the bridegroom tarried, they all slumbered and slept. And at midnight there was a cry made, Behold, the bridegroom cometh; go ye out to meet him. Then all those virgins arose and trimmed their lamps. And the foolish said unto the wise, Give us of your oil; for our lamps are gone out. But the wise answered, saying, Not so, lest there be not enough for us and you; but go rather to them that sell, and buy for yourselves. And while they went to buy, the bridegroom came, and they that were ready went in with him to the marriage; and the door was shut. Afterward came also the other virgins, saying, Lord, Lord, open to us. But he answered and said, Verily I say unto you, I know you not. Watch, therefore; for ye know neither the day nor the hour in which the Son of man cometh."

This parable is intended to teach us about the suddenness and unexpectedness of the Lord's coming. It calls for us to be prepared for that unknown moment.

A. The Subject of the Parable

Verse 1 begins with the word *then*. Christ is referring to a specific time: His second coming, which He is talking about in the closing verses of Matthew 24. He was speaking of when He comes to reward the faithful servant and punish the unfaithful servant. The parable of the ten virgins tells us what will happen when the kingdom comes. It is a simple parable; it tells us that Christ will come at an unexpected moment to judge sinners and reward the righteous. Afterward there will be no second chance. People may knock on the door of the kingdom all they want to, but the door will remain shut.

B. The Simplicity of the Parable

The parable of the ten virgins, although simple, can be confusing when one reads what commentaries have to say about it. Some turn the parable into an allegory and give everything a mystical meaning with secret spiritual applications. Others try to make every element of the parable applicable to the Christian life. Still others try to analyze the data in the parable and say it's confusing because there's a bridegroom and ten bridesmaids but no bride. They ask, "Were the bridesmaids waiting at the bride's house or the groom's house? Did they sleep outside on the street or in the house? How could young maidens carry the heavy lamps?" But those things need to be set aside. We need to stick to the text; in fact, there are only four things we need to understand: the wedding, the bridesmaids, the bridegroom, and the warning.

Lesson

I. THE WEDDING (v. 1)

Jesus depicts a wedding in His parable. In Bible times, weddings were a village event. They were the greatest social celebration. Everyone got involved: friends, families, and neighbors. They were a time of happiness and festivity.

A. The Arrangement of a Marriage

There were three elements in a Jewish marriage of that time.

1. The engagement

The couple to be married would become engaged long before the actual wedding. The fathers who were giving their children in marriage made an official contract with each other. Thus engagements weren't made by the couple; they were made by the fathers.

2. The betrothal

The betrothal was an official ceremony. The couple would come together before friends and family to make binding vows. They were then considered officially married. If the betrothal was broken, the couple was considered divorced (cf. Matt. 1:18-19). And if the husband died during the betrothal, the wife was considered a widow—even though the marriage had not been consummated. The betrothal period gave the young man up to a year to get ready for the responsibility of having a wife. He had to provide a place for her. He would either add onto his father's house or build his own house. He had to purchase land and cultivate a field to show he could provide for her.

3. The wedding

At the end of the betrothal period, the bridegroom would take his bride to live with him. This was accompanied by a big celebration. It's this element of the marriage that the parable focuses on.

The Jewish people had a good system for setting up marriages. Parents often had more wisdom and long-range perception than their children about prospective spouses and married life. Having the couple express their vows to one another at the betrothal involved commitment. A man didn't have to worry about getting everything prepared for his bride only to have her say, "I don't know how to tell you this, but I've found someone else." Likewise, the woman was assured of not being forsaken. Betrothals were binding. Any preparation the couple put into the marriage would lead to fulfillment.

B. The Anticipation Before a Marriage

You can imagine the anticipation of the bride and bridegroom as they waited for the marriage to begin. That's what we see in the parable of the ten virgins. The wedding celebration started when the bridegroom came to the bride's house. The bride and all the bridesmaids would be there waiting for him. Then they would all go through the village at night with torches in a celebration of singing, talking, and joy unequaled in any other social event. In the parable, everything was ready for the wedding to start. The bridegroom had prepared a home. He was now coming to come take his bride to their new home. He would come at night so that the procession through the village could be enjoyed by everyone. Then the wedding party would go to the couple's house, where the celebration would continue for as long as seven days. At the end of the celebration, a friend of the bridegroom would take the hand of the bride, place it in the hand of the bridegroom, and everyone would leave. Then the couple would consummate their marriage.

II. THE BRIDESMAIDS (vv. 1-5)

A. Their Supplies

Matthew 25:1 introduces us to ten virgins with lamps. The Greek word translated "lamps" actually means "torches." Christ wasn't talking about the kind of lamp that is mentioned in Matthew 5:15, which can be hidden under a bushel. He was talking about a torch—like the ones that were used in John 18:3 by the Roman soldiers who arrested Jesus in the Garden of Gethsemane. These torches were long wooden poles that had some kind of wire mesh attached to the end, filled with cloth. That cloth would be soaked in oil and then lit. When people used those torches, they carried a little flask of oil with them so they could keep the torch lit as long as necessary. So the ten bridesmaids were at the house of the bride with their torches, waiting for the bridegroom to come.

B. Their Status

1. Socially

   a) The selection of virgin bridesmaids

   In the parable, the bridesmaids are called "virgins" (Gk., *parthenos*), which refers to an unmarried girl who is a virgin. People married young in Bible times, and often the bridesmaids were young girls who were sisters, cousins, or intimate friends of the bride. It was a privilege for them to attend the bride and wait in anticipation of the glorious evening when the bridegroom would come.

b) The significance of virgin bridesmaids

There's nothing significant about the bridesmaids being virgins. Jesus wasn't saying that all ten girls were moral people. Their virginity was not symbolic of their spiritual state. Jesus called them virgins simply because bridesmaids were usually virgins.

c) The sum of virgin bridesmaids

Notice also that there were ten virgins. Apparently the Jews favored the number *ten*. Josephus said there had to be at least ten men assembled to partake of a paschal lamb (*Wars* VI.ix.3). Ten men had to be present at a wedding to give the proper blessing. It took ten men to constitute a synagogue. Apparently ten bridesmaids was a customary number to have.

All ten bridesmaids carried torches, just as bridesmaids today carry flowers to show they are part of a wedding party. They waited in anticipation of meeting the bridegroom. The Greek word translated "meet" in Matthew 25:1 refers to greeting an official dignitary. It's an official term appropriate for the event.

2. Spiritually

a) The outward appearance

Who was Christ referring to when He spoke of the ten virgins? It's obvious from the context He was talking about people who profess to be Christians— to be part of the church. They say they know Christ, and they anticipate His coming. They even say they are prepared for Him; they have on their wedding garments and have their torches. Their presence symbolizes their interest in Christ, and their torches symbolize their profession of faith in Christ. They show outward marks of watching for the coming of the bridegroom: Christ. They are gathered as bridesmaids, waiting to be received into the glorious marriage celebration.

b) The inward reality

On the surface the ten bridesmaids are indistinguishable. Yet they are not alike. Verse 2 says "five of them were wise [Gk., *phronimos*, "thoughtful, sensible, prudent"], and five were foolish [Gk., *moros*, "moron, stupid"]." It may not be clear which is which, but He who searches men's hearts knows (1 Sam. 16:7). Bible commentator William Arnot said, "There is not a more grand or a more beautiful spectacle on earth than a great assembly reverently worshipping God together. No line visible to human eye divides into two parts the goodly company; yet the goodly company is divided into two parts. The Lord reads our character and marks our place. The Lord knows them that are his, and them that are not his, in every assembly of worshippers" (*The Parables of Our Lord* [London: Nelson, 1869], p. 290). The Lord can look at all those who go to church and profess to be Christians and know who is truly His and who isn't—who is wise and who isn't. Wisdom or foolishness manifests itself in how prepared you are for Christ's return.

Matthew 25:3-4 says, "They that were foolish took their lamps, and took no oil with them; but the wise took oil in their vessels with their lamps." The foolish had no oil, so they were not prepared for Christ's return. Their attachment to Christ was merely external. They hadn't secured the most important thing of all: the oil necessary to light the torch.

The oil represents saving grace. In a crowd of people who outwardly appear to honor Christ will be some whose hearts are unprepared. They have not received salvation by grace. The oil in this parable is reminiscent of the wedding garment in Matthew 22:11. At his son's wedding a king found a guest without a wedding garment and kicked him out. The man was unprepared to enter God's kingdom; he had not prepared his heart.

Paul told Timothy there are some people who have a form of godliness but without power (2 Tim. 3:5). The foolish virgins were like that. They were committed to Christ intellectually, socially, and religiously. However, they had no light or life. They had no ability to be conformed to the law of God. Their faith was dead (cf. James 2:17); it showed no fruit. Christ warns us in Matthew 25 not to be like the unprepared virgins.

An Unpopular Message

Throughout His ministry, Christ repeatedly warned that people who are not saved will be attaching themselves to the church. For example, He said that in His kingdom on earth would grow both wheat and tares. He warned they would look so much alike that we are not to pull out the tares lest we pull out the wheat (Matt. 13:28-29). The separation of the two will take place when the Lord returns (v. 30). In another parable in Matthew 13 He says that seeds will be planted in what appears to be good soil, but later on they will be strangled by weeds or have their roots stunted by rocks. Such plants won't bear fruit and will die. But initially you can't tell that what appears to be a healthy plant will later die off. The Lord is saying that churches everywhere will be filled with people who are not saved and not prepared for His return.

Some people wonder if there is any significance about there being five wise virgins and five foolish ones. I don't think the Lord was saying that half of those who profess to be Christians aren't really saved. He was simply pointing out that there are many unredeemed people in the church. There are many who are unprepared to meet the Lord upon death or at the time of the second coming. Some of them will deceive themselves by thinking that everything is all right because they are involved in church. People don't like being confronted with the possibility that they aren't saved. I wrote an article about that subject for a magazine, and the publishers didn't publish it because they said it would upset people. But the Lord warned people to be prepared because He doesn't want people to be self-deceived and go to hell.

C. Their Slumber

1. Christ's remark about a long wait

   Jesus says in Matthew 25:5, "While the bridegroom tarried, they all slumbered and slept." Apparently the bridegroom didn't come when the bridesmaids expected him. Perhaps the Lord was subtly telling the disciples that the kingdom wouldn't come immediately as they thought it would. There would be a long wait. Matthew 25:5 also indicates that even when the signs that precede Christ's coming have been fulfilled, there will be a lapse of time before He returns. People will be waiting for Him, and when they see nothing happening, they will say, "Nothing's going to happen. We may as well get back into our normal routines again." In a sense, they will fall asleep. They may have been excited at first, just as people are on the day before a wedding. However, the bridesmaids waited so long that they fell asleep.

   Notice that both the wise and the foolish virgins were asleep. So there wasn't anything wrong with being asleep. It's just that the wise virgins were already prepared before they fell asleep. They were ready for whatever might come when they woke up. But the foolish were caught unprepared. They should have got oil for their lamps while they had the opportunity. Their false security let them sleep through the day of opportunity.

2. Christian responsibility during the long wait

   As we wait for the Lord to return, we can't be standing on our tiptoes every moment looking for Him. Life has to go on. Yet just because we continue to carry on with life doesn't mean we've stopped waiting. We are to wait as we carry out our daily responsibilities. Remember what we read in Matthew 24:40-41: "Then shall two be in the field; the one shall be taken, and the other left. Two women shall be grinding at the mill; the one shall be taken, and the other left." People will be carrying on business as usual when Christ returns. As Matthew 24:38 says, it will be as it was in the days of Noah, when people kept on eating, drinking, and marrying.

III. THE BRIDEGROOM (vv. 6-12)

A. The Arrival

Matthew 25:6 begins, "At midnight there was a cry made." Apparently the bridegroom tarried a long time. Midnight is a late time to start a wedding. The point our Lord wanted to make is that He will return at an unexpected time. We now understand why the bridesmaids fell asleep: most people are asleep by midnight. No one would expect a wedding to start that late. We learn from Exodus 12:29-33 that the deliverance of Israel from Egypt also took place at midnight. Many rabbis used to say that when the Messiah came, it would be at midnight.

First Thessalonians 5:2 says Christ will come as a thief in the night. The world will somehow be lulled into complacency, and the Lord will come at an unexpected moment— even after all the signs preceding His return have been fulfilled. The bridesmaids knew the wedding was near; they could read the signs. They knew it was time to gather at the bride's house, but five of them wasted their opportunity to be prepared. Then came the cry at midnight—the cry that announced His approach.

Matthew 25:6 tells us of the cry: "Behold, the bridegroom cometh; go ye out to meet him." That glorious moment began the wedding, and the celebration would go on for several days. In Jewish wedding tradition, the bridegroom would come to the bride's house with his groomsmen. The bride and the ten bridesmaids would join them, and the procession would begin. The bridesmaids would set afire their torches to light the way back to the groom's house. This moment in the wedding is analogous to the moment of Christ's second coming.

B. The Awakening

In verse 7 Jesus says, "Then all those virgins arose and trimmed their lamps." They probably had to get the cloth at the end of the torch ready to receive the oil. Those who had oil with them poured it on the cloth and lit their torches. Those who didn't have oil now realized they were unprepared. But they hadn't anticipated that the bridegroom would come when it was too late to buy any oil. They were unprepared. The apostle Paul wrote, "Examine yourselves, whether you are in the faith" (2 Cor. 13:5). He challenged us to make sure we are saved. When the bridegroom arrived, the truth was revealed: they were unprepared. They had no oil (internal holiness) and therefore couldn't light their torches.

C. The Appeal

What did the foolish virgins do when they realized they had no oil? Matthew 25:8 says, "The foolish said unto the wise, Give us of your oil; for our lamps are gone out." According to the Greek text, the phrase translated "our lamps are gone out" could be read "our lamps are going out." Apparently the foolish virgins tried to light their torches using only the cloth. But without oil, the cloth could only smolder a little while before the flame went out. So they asked the wise virgins for some oil.

It's Up to You

If you're called to the judgment seat of God—whether at death or the second coming—no one can help you. All the saints in heaven and the believers on earth could weep on your behalf but that wouldn't save you. Salvation is nontransferable. As we will see in a moment, the wise virgins didn't give any oil to the foolish ones. That's not because they were selfish; it's just that an unbeliever can't ask a believer for salvation. Every person is accountable to make his own life right before God.

D. The Answer

The answer from the wise virgins appears in verse 9: "Not so, lest there be not enough for us and you; but go rather to them that sell, and buy for yourselves." That the foolish virgins are told to buy oil doesn't mean salvation can be bought. It's a free gift (Rom. 6:23). But there is a price: you have to give up your very self. That's illustrated in Matthew 13:45-46, where a merchant sold everything he had to buy a great pearl. Isaiah 55:1 confirms that salvation must be procured on your own: "Every one that thirsteth, come to the waters, and he that hath no money; come, buy and eat; yea, come buy wine and milk without money and without price."

No one can give you salvation. You have to go to God on your own. The foolish virgins had the opportunity to get oil, but they slept it away. They weren't allowed to be a part of the wedding ceremony without a lit torch. They didn't have what was necessary.

Salvation: Going, Going, Gone!

One of the most fearful teachings in the Bible is that there is coming a day when it will be too late for unbelievers to become saved. Jesus taught repeatedly that there are myriads of people attaching themselves to the church who are unprepared to face God. They are self-deceived about their status with God. When they finally realize they are unprepared, it will be too late to do anything. In Luke 6:46-49 Jesus says, "Why call ye me, Lord, Lord, and do not the things which I say? Whosoever cometh to me, and heareth my sayings, and doeth them, I will show you to whom he is like: He is like a man who built an house, and dug deep, and laid the foundation on a rock; and when the flood arose, the stream beat vehemently upon that house, and could not shake it; for it was founded upon a rock. But he that heareth, and doeth not, is like a man that, without a foundation, built an house upon the earth, against which the stream did beat vehemently, and immediately it fell; and the ruin of that house was great."

There are people who have built their religious house but have no foundation. The resident holiness of God isn't there. There's no transformed character. Just because such a person says he's a Christian and goes to church doesn't mean he is saved. We need to be prepared internally.

E. The Abandoning

1. The reception into the kingdom

In verse 10 we read that while the foolish virgins went to get oil "the bridegroom came, and they that were ready went in with him to the marriage; and the door was shut." There was no place for the foolish virgins to buy oil at midnight. While they were gone, the door to the wedding was shut. Imagine the sheer terror of those who will face God someday, realizing that they have been caught unprepared and the door to the kingdom is shut. They will feel the same way the evil people of Noah's day did when the floodwaters began to rise and they couldn't get into the ark.

2. The rejection from the kingdom

The door into the kingdom is open now. But someday it will be shut. Some people will be caught unprepared. They will have been given a chance beforehand. They will see the signs during the Tribulation. They will see the sign of the Son of Man in heaven. But then they'll go to sleep when they should be getting prepared. The same applies to all unbelievers who die before the second coming. They will stand before God unprepared. They will know the same shock as those who appear before the Lord in Matthew 7:22-23: "Many will say to me in that day, Lord, Lord, have we not prophesied in thy name? And in thy name have cast out demons? And in thy name done many wonderful works? And then will I profess unto them, I never knew you; depart from me, ye that work iniquity."

The church is filled with people who are not ready. Jesus gives a warning to such people in Luke 13: "Strive to enter in at the narrow gate; for many, I say unto you, will seek to enter in, and shall not be able. When once the master of the house is risen up, and hath shut the door, and ye begin to stand outside, and to knock at the door, saying, Lord, Lord, open unto us; and he shall answer and say unto you, I know you not from where ye are; then shall ye begin to say, We have eaten and have drunk in thy presence, and thou hast taught in our streets. But he shall say, I tell you, I know you not from where ye are; depart from me, all ye workers of iniquity. There shall be weeping and gnashing of teeth" (vv. 24-28).

In Matthew 25:11-12 we read, "Afterward came also the other virgins, saying, Lord, Lord, open to us. But he answered and said, Verily I say unto you, I know you not." There's no second chance. The only way you can make sure you are ready for the Lord's return is to be ready every day. You never know when you might die. There is no getting around the inevitable hour of judgment. If you are caught unprepared, the door of the kingdom will be forever closed to you.

IV. THE WARNING (v. 13)

The parable concludes, "Watch, therefore; for ye know neither the day nor the hour in which the Son of man cometh" (v. 13). No one knows the exact moment of the second coming. We know the era: it will be right after the Tribulation. It will be after the signs in Matthew 24 and after the sign of the Son of Man in heaven. But how much time will pass after that before the Lord comes? No one knows. So be ready now. Even if you're only a little too late, you will be too late forever.

Luke 21:34-36 repeats the same warning: "Take heed to yourselves, lest at any time your hearts be overcharged with surfeiting, and drunkenness, and cares of this life, and so that day come upon you unawares. For like a snare shall it come on all them that dwell on the face of the whole earth. Watch ye, therefore, and pray always, that ye may be accounted worthy to escape all these things that shall come to pass, and to stand before the Son of man."

Conclusion

Don't be caught unprepared. That's the message in the parable of the ten virgins. Nineteenth-century English poet Alfred Tennyson in his *Idylls of the King* adapted that parable to write this for Queen Guinevere, who learned too late the cost of sin:

> Late, late, so late! and dark the night and chill!
> Late, late, so late! but we can enter still.
> Too late, too late! ye cannot enter now.
>
> No light had we: for that we do repent;
> And learning this, the bridegroom will relent.
> Too late, too late! ye cannot enter now.

No light: so late! and dark and chill the night!
O let us in, that we may find the light!
Too late, too late: ye cannot enter now.

Have we not heard the bridegroom is so sweet?
O let us in, tho' late, to kiss his feet!
No, no, too late! ye cannot enter now.

Focusing on the Facts

1. What is the subject of the parable of the ten virgins (see pp. 148-49)?
2. What were the three elements of a Jewish marriage in Christ's time? Which element is focused on in the parable (see pp. 149-50)?
3. Is it significant that the bridesmaids were virgins? Explain (see p. 152).
4. Who do the bridesmaids symbolize (see pp. 152-53)?
5. In what way were the bridesmaids similar? How were they different (see p. 153)?
6. In the parable, what does the oil represent (see p. 153)?
7. What does Christ teach about the church in Matthew 13 (see p. 154)?
8. What happened to the virgins as they waited for the bridegroom? Was there anything wrong with that? What had the foolish virgins done that *was* wrong (see p. 155)?
9. What is the Christian's responsibility as he awaits the Lord's return (see p. 155)?
10. What appeal do the foolish virgins make to the wise virgins in Matthew 25:8? What answer did the wise virgins give? What was Jesus illustrating in that dialogue (see pp. 157-58)?
11. What will happen to those who are caught unprepared when the Lord sets up His kingdom (see pp. 158-59)?
12. What is the only way we can make sure we are ready for the Lord's return (see p. 160)?

Pondering the Principles

1. In the parable of the ten virgins, Christ confirms that salvation is a matter between you and God. It is nontransferable. Read Ne-

hemiah 9:1-3, Psalm 139:23-24, and Romans 6:12-13. Who is responsible for our sin? What is the source of forgiveness, according to Isaiah 43:15, 25 and Jeremiah 31:34? Unless you have confessed your sins to God and repented, asking Christ to become Lord of your life, you are not prepared for Christ's return. And if you are already a Christian, it's important to "let your light so shine before men, that they may see your good works, and glorify your Father, who is in heaven" (Matt. 5:16). There's great joy in being prepared for Christ's return, as there is much to anticipate in the coming kingdom!

2. In Romans 13:12-14, the apostle Paul encourages us to watch and be ready for the Lord's return. Meditate on these verses, and determine how God would want you to apply them: "The night is far spent, the day is at hand; let us, therefore, cast off the works of darkness, and let us put on the armor of light. Let us walk honestly, as in the day; not in reveling and drunkenness, not in immorality and wantonness, not in strife and envying. But put ye on the Lord Jesus Christ, and make not provision for the flesh, to fulfill its lusts."

11
The Tragedy of Wasted Opportunity—Part 1

Outline

Introduction

Lesson
I. The Responsibility We Receive (vv. 14-15)
   A. The Picture
      1. The recipients of responsibility
      2. The rendering of responsibility
   B. The Portioning
      1. Explaining what was apportioned
      2. Examining how it was apportioned
   C. The Parallel
II. The Reaction We Have (vv. 16-18)
   A. How a True Believer Will Respond (vv. 16-17)
   B. How an Unbeliever Will Respond (v. 18)
III. The Reckoning We Face (vv. 19-27)
   A. The Return (v. 19)
      1. What the Master will do when He returns
      2. When the Master will return
   B. The Reckoning (vv. 20-27)
      1. Of the faithful (vv. 20-23)
      2. Of the unfaithful (vv. 24-27)
         a) The servant's remark (vv. 24-25)
         b) The master's response (vv. 26-27)

Introduction

God calls us to make the most of the spiritual opportunities available to us. He wants us to maximize our privileges. Ecclesiastes 11 says, "Cast thy bread upon the waters; for thou shalt find it after many days. . . . In the morning sow thy seed, and in the evening withhold not thine hand; for thou knowest not which shall prosper, either this or that" (vv. 1, 6). We are to aggressively pursue our opportunities. Proverbs 10:5 says, "He that gathereth in summer is a wise son, but he that sleepeth in harvest is a son that causeth shame." Gather the harvest when it's there; don't wait until it's too late. In Psalm 69:13 David says, "As for me, my prayer is unto thee, O Lord, in an acceptable time." Isaiah wrote, "Seek ye the Lord while he may be found, call ye upon him while he is near" (Isa. 55:6).

Jeremiah said, "The stork in the heaven knoweth her appointed times, and the turtle and the crane and the swallow observe the time of their coming, but my people know not the law of the Lord" (Jer. 8:7). The animals know how to take care of themselves in certain seasons, yet some people don't know what God wants them to know. Psalm 95:6-8 says, "Come, let us worship and bow down; let us kneel before the Lord our maker. For he is our God, and we are the people of his pasture, and the sheep of his hand. Today if ye will hear his voice, harden not your heart" (cf. Heb. 3:7-8). Paul wrote, "Behold, now is the accepted time; behold, now is the day of salvation" (2 Cor. 6:2).

Even the Lord Jesus called us to make the most of our spiritual opportunities. In John 12:35-36 He says, "Yet a little while is the light with you. Walk while ye have the light, lest darkness come upon you; for he that walketh in darkness knoweth not where he goeth. While ye have light, believe in the light, that ye may be the sons of light." Nineteenth-century American poet John Greenleaf Whittier wrote, "For all sad words of tongue or pen, the saddest are these: 'It might have been!'" (*Maud Muller,* 1.105). The tragedy of wasted opportunity—that's the theme of the parable in Matthew 25:14-30.

Lesson

Let's read the parable of the talents so we can construct a picture of what's happening before we examine it in detail. Jesus said, "The kingdom of heaven is like a man traveling into a far country, who called his own servants, and delivered unto them his goods. And unto one he gave five talents, to another two, and to another one, to every man according to his ability; and straightway took his journey. Then he that had received the five talents went and traded with the same, and made other five talents. And likewise he that had received two, he also gained other two. But he that had received one went and dug in the earth, and hid his lord's money.

"After a long time the lord of those servants cometh, and reckoneth with them. And so he that had received five talents came and brought other five talents, saying, Lord, thou deliveredst unto me five talents; behold, I have gained beside them five talents more. His lord said unto him, Well done, thou good and faithful servant; thou hast been faithful over a few things, I will make thee ruler over many things. Enter thou into the joy of thy lord. He also that had received two talents came and said, Lord, thou deliveredst unto me two talents; behold, I have gained two other talents beside them. His lord said unto him, Well done, good and faithful servant; thou hast been faithful over a few things, I will make thee ruler over many things. Enter thou into the joy of thy lord.

"Then he that had received the one talent came and said, Lord, I knew thee, that thou art an hard man, reaping where thou hast not sown, and gathering where thou hast not spread, and I was afraid, and went and hid thy talent in the earth; lo, there thou hast what is thine. His lord answered and said unto him, Thou wicked and slothful servant, thou knewest that I reap where I sowed not, and gather where I have not spread? Thou oughtest, therefore, to have put my money to the exchangers, and then, at my coming, I should have received mine own with interest. Take, therefore, the talent from him, and give it unto him who hath ten talents. For unto every one that hath shall be given, and he shall have abundance; but from him that hath not shall be taken away even that which he hath. And cast the unprofitable servant into outer darkness; there shall be weeping and gnashing of teeth" (Matt. 25:14-30).

That is a parable about wasted opportunity. It is not the same parable recorded in Luke 19:11-27. That parable was taught several days earlier, before Christ's triumphal entry, and is distinctly different. As we examine Matthew 25:14-30, I'll break it down into four basic points that illustrate what we need to know about spiritual opportunity: the responsibility we receive, the reaction we have, the reckoning we face, and the reward we gain.

I. THE RESPONSIBILITY WE RECEIVE (vv. 14-15)

Verse 14 begins with the phrase "the kingdom of heaven." Some Bibles place that in italics. That restates what verse 1 says: that these parables teach what will happen when Christ's kingdom comes to earth. In the Greek text, the transition that appears between the two parables indicates Jesus is still talking about the same subject He has been in verses 1-13.

What Exactly Is the Kingdom of Heaven?

In Matthew 25 Jesus teaches two parables about the kingdom. Basically the kingdom is the sphere of salvation and all that it entails. But more specifically, the kingdom of heaven can be understood in two ways:

1. Its internal, invisible sense

Sometimes the phrase "the kingdom of heaven" refers to the body of redeemed people who live on the earth. God rules in the lives of His people. In Matthew 18:3 we read, "Except ye be converted, and become as little children, ye shall not enter into the kingdom of heaven." A person cannot enter the kingdom of heaven unless he becomes a believer. In Matthew 25:34 Jesus again speaks of the kingdom in that manner: "Inherit the kingdom prepared for you from the foundation of the world."

2. Its external, organizational sense

The phrase "the kingdom of heaven" also refers to all those who identify themselves with Christ. Some are true believers and some are false. The parable of the wheat and the tares in Matthew 13 illustrates that (vv. 24-30). In Matthew 13:47-50 the kingdom is compared to a dragnet that picks up both good and bad creatures from the sea. The good ones will be kept, and the bad ones thrown away.

In the parable of the ten virgins, we saw that five of the virgins possessed God's saving grace, but five didn't. They all identified themselves with Christ externally, but only five were really believers. Thus that parable talked about the external aspect of the kingdom. The parable of the talents does likewise.

The word *church* is used in the same two ways. Sometimes when we talk about the church, we are talking about the collective body of those who are truly redeemed. Other times we are talking about everyone who identifies himself with the church as an organization. In every church you will find a mixture of true believers and those who profess to be believers but aren't.

A. The Picture

Jesus began the parable of the talents by saying, "The kingdom of heaven is like a man traveling into a far country, who called his own servants, and delivered unto them his goods." In Bible times, going to a far country could mean a trip of up to one or two years in length. When a person was to be gone that long, he would entrust his servants with his personal and business matters. And just as this man had a group of servants, there are different kinds of servants in the external kingdom.

The way the servants managed their master's assets while he was on his trip showed what kind of servants they were. This parable can be applied to all who externally identify themselves with Christ's church. The way they use the resources God has given them will show if their hearts are right or not.

1. The recipients of responsibility

Notice in verse 14 that the master "called his *own* servants" (emphasis added). He is familiar with these servants; they identify themselves with him. Yet they could be either good or bad servants.

2. The rendering of responsibility

Verse 14 concludes by saying that the master "delivered unto them his goods." Because he will be gone for a long time, he needs to make sure his business matters are taken care of. He needs to make wise investments so that his money will keep up with the economy, and he needs to make sure his crops are sown and harvested. Everything has to be cared for.

The word translated "servants" in verse 14 is the Greek word *doulos*. Although *doulos* can refer to servants who are slaves, that's not always the case. The Greek word *doulos* can be translated "employee" in this parable. The servants in the parable were most likely artists, craftsmen, traders, and people who had a good mind for business. Those are the kind of people a householder would entrust his estate to when he went on a trip. In those days, servants were frequently given a certain amount of goods with the idea that they would earn a profit or interest on the property by the time the master came back.

B. The Portioning

Verse 15 says that "unto one he gave five talents, to another two, and to another one, to every man according to his ability." Since the master was familiar with his servants, he gave each one what he thought he could handle.

1. Explaining what was apportioned

In English, we use the word *talent* to refer to someone's skills. But in the Bible, a talent was a specific weight. In Revelation 16:21 we read of hailstones "about the weight of a talent." The value of each talent depended on what kind of metal it was. A talent of gold would be worth a lot of money. A talent of silver would be worth less, and a talent of copper even less. The talents mentioned in Matthew 25 were most likely made of silver, since the word *money* in verse 18 is translated from a Greek word that was frequently used to refer to silver coinage.

2. Examining how it was apportioned

The talents were probably put in bags. One bag weighed five talents, another two talents, and another one talent. The servants were to invest the money and receive a return on it. By doing so, they would show they were faithful stewards. And it's not really important how much money each servant was given. What's important is how each servant handled the money. They were given amounts according to their ability. The one who received five talents apparently had greater capacity to handle a larger amount of money than the other two servants.

C. The Parallel

In the parable, the master represents our Lord. He is currently away on a journey—He is waiting in heaven until His second coming. We who are in the church are the servants who have been entrusted with bags of money. We are to use what we are given the way God wants us to until Christ returns. We have varying amounts of resources entrusted to us because each of us was created with different capabilities and we exist in differing circumstances. Some Christians have doctorate degrees from seminaries and others know only the gospel message itself. That we're all different is all right; it's by God's design. Some of us have been given five talents from the Lord and others only one.

If a servant really loves his master, he's going to take advantage of his opportunity to bring a return on his master's resources. The Lord gives everyone in the church the opportunity to use His resources. The issue is how you use that opportunity. Among the many resources God has given us are the abilities to teach, evangelize the lost, and minister to the needy. Do you utilize them? Do you take advantage of all that God offers to you for the sake of His kingdom?

Those of us who go to good churches with extensive ministries carry a heavier bag than those who live in places with little or no opportunities. We need to use the resources God has made available to us. There are some Christians who don't know any other Christians in their family or community. There are even some towns, cities, or countries in the world where Christians are few and far between. Wherever you are, God has put you there because

He knows what your capabilities are. He will give you responsibilities that match up with them.

Just because we are given differing abilities doesn't mean we are limited as to the results we can produce. In verses 16-17 of the parable we learn that the servants with five and two talents each received a 100 percent return on their investments. The point is that the Lord wants us to be faithful with what He has given us. And every time you learn something new or a new opportunity comes your way, your bag becomes heavier.

II. THE REACTION WE HAVE (vv. 16-18)

A. How a True Believer Will Respond (vv. 16-17)

In verse 16 Jesus says, "He that had received the five talents went and traded with the same, and made other five talents." Apparently the servant immediately put his master's money to work. An immediate response is a sign of true salvation. The servant's heart immediately responded to the privilege of serving his lord.

The servant "traded with" his five talents. He went out and did business. The parable doesn't tell exactly what he did. It may be that he bought a field, cultivated it, and produced a crop worth twice as much as he paid for the field. He may have bought a piece of land, then turned around and sold it at a profit. It's possible he used the money to buy and trade some kind of commodity. The key is that he gained another five talents. The word translated "made" is the Greek word *kerdainō*, which means "to profit." He gained five more talents, thus doubling his master's money. He showed maximum commitment in caring for his master's resources. Likewise we are to make the most of our spiritual privileges.

Matthew 25:17 tells us that the man who received two talents also gained another two. He made the most of what he was given. He didn't have as much as the man with five talents, but he got a 100 percent return. Likewise, some of us may not have as many opportunities as others, but we can still give God a maximum return on the privileges He has given us. Regardless of how much you are entrusted with, the point is to maximize your opportunities.

B. How an Unbeliever Will Respond (v. 18)

In Matthew 25:18 we read that the servant who received one talent "went and dug in the earth, and hid his lord's money." In those days people commonly stored money in the ground. Matthew 13:44 relates a parable about a man who found a treasure in a field. Apparently the money had been hidden for safekeeping. An Israelite named Achan took some treasures from the conquest of Jericho and hid them in the ground under his tent (Josh. 7:21). The servant in Matthew 25 buried the one talent entrusted to him and wasted the opportunity to make a return on his master's money.

Jesus wasn't saying that those who are entrusted with little things will be unfaithful. He's saying that even if you only have a little entrusted to you, you are responsible for it. No matter how much God has given you, you're responsible to give God a return. There are some people whom God has given privilege after privilege, yet they let it all go to waste. Some people with five talents envision themselves as true servants yet are really doing nothing for God. Others have been given little but use it well. Perhaps Jesus used the man with the one talent to represent the wicked servant to show that the master's anger wasn't related to how much money was lost. The master was angry because the servant wasted his opportunity.

We are all equally responsible for the spiritual privileges God has given us. We have been given different kinds of opportunities, but we are to do our best to get a maximum return.

III. THE RECKONING WE FACE (vv. 19-27)

A. The Return (v. 19)

1. What the Master will do when He returns

Jesus says in verse 19, "After a long time the lord of those servants cometh, and reckoneth with them." The word translated "reckon" is a commercial term meaning "to compare accounts." The master of the household returned from his trip and looked at his records to see how his servants did with their resources. That's what will happen to all people when the Lord returns. He will take a look at the books to see what men have done with their opportunity to serve the Lord. What are you doing with the spiritual privileges you have? Are you serving the Lord as you should?

2. When the Master will return

Notice that verse 19 says the master returned "after a long time." Again the Lord was trying to tell the disciples that His second coming will not happen as soon as they thought it would. That's what is implied in Matthew 25:5 in the parable of the ten virgins when He said that the bridegroom tarried late. Jesus didn't tell the disciples how much of a delay there would be; He didn't want them to stop serving in anticipation of His coming.

Are You too Preoccupied with the Second Coming?

In the 1970s many people in the evangelical church became preoccupied with the second coming of Christ. I remember talking to some people who had sold their property. One man in particular liquidated $500,000 worth of assets to buy New Testaments, little praying hands that glow in the dark, and pictures of Jesus. He shipped them all over the world. He ended up going bankrupt as he prepared for the second coming. Paul rebuked the Thessalonians for neglecting their earthly responsibilities while they awaited the Lord's return (2 Thess. 3:6-13). That's what was happening a few years ago. People didn't plan for the future because they thought the Lord would return any minute. However, we don't want to be guilty of going to the other extreme and saying that the Lord won't be returning for some time to come.

When the Lord returns, He will separate the true from the false. And He will look at the books to see how we managed His assets. Let's take a quick look at what the master of the household did when he reckoned with his servants.

B. The Reckoning (vv. 20-27)

1. Of the faithful (vv. 20-23)

   Matthew 25:20-23 says, "He that had received five talents came and brought other five talents, saying, Lord,
   thou deliveredst unto me five talents; behold, I have
   gained beside them five talents more. His lord said unto
   him, Well done, thou good and faithful servant; thou
   hast been faithful over a few things, I will make thee ruler over many things. Enter thou into the joy of thy lord.
   He also that had received two talents came and said,
   Lord, thou deliveredst unto me two talents; behold, I
   have gained two other talents beside them. His lord said
   unto him, Well done, good and faithful servant; thou
   hast been faithful over a few things, I will make thee ruler over many things. Enter thou into the joy of thy
   lord." Those two servants gave a full return on the opportunity given to them. They represent true believers—genuine servants of God. They are the sheep
   mentioned in Matthew 25:32-40.

2. Of the unfaithful (vv. 24-27)

   a) The servant's remark (vv. 24-25)

      After telling about the master's response to the two
      faithful servants, Jesus tells us about the exchange
      between the master and the man who was given one
      talent: "He that had received the one talent came and
      said, Lord, I knew thee, that thou art an hard man,
      reaping where thou hast not sown, and gathering
      where thou hast not spread, and I was afraid, and
      went and hid thy talent in the earth; lo, there thou
      hast what is thine."

   b) The master's response (vv. 26-27)

      When the master heard the servant's words, he said,
      "Thou wicked and slothful servant." The master was
      upset because the servant failed to take advantage of
      the opportunity that was given to him.

In the next lesson, we'll be taking a closer look at the significance of the servants' responses. But this much is clear: two of the servants in the parable used their opportunities to serve the Lord, and by doing so, proved that their salvation was genuine. They were willing to spend their time for His sake. One servant didn't use his spiritual privilege. Instead, he hid it in the ground and spent his time doing what he wanted to do. He called himself a servant, but he wasn't one. He said he belonged to the master, but he didn't and was ultimately thrown out. Christ was warning us again about the importance of demonstrating that you belong to His kingdom. It's not enough to just identify with it outwardly.

Focusing on the Facts

1. What exhortations are we given in Isaiah 55:6 and Psalm 95:6-8 (see p. 164)?
2. What two things can the phrase "the kingdom of heaven" refer to in the New Testament? In which way is it used in the parables of the ten virgins and the talents (see pp. 166-67)?
3. Why did the master entrust his servants with the care of his possessions? What did he expect the servants to do with them (see pp. 167-68)?
4. Why were the servants given different amounts (see p. 169)?
5. What will a servant who loves his master do when he is entrusted with his master's possessions (see p. 169)?
6. Does having only a little to be responsible for limit us to the results we can produce? Explain (see p. 170).
7. What kind of return did the servants with five talents and two talents receive on their master's money (see p. 170)?
8. Regardless of how much you are _____ with, the point is to _____ your opportunities (see p. 171).
9. What did the man with one talent do with the money? Was that unusual? Explain (see p. 171).
10. Is Jesus saying in verse 18 that there is a relationship between being entrusted with little things and being an unfaithful steward? Explain (see p. 171).

11. According to Matthew 25:19, what did the master do when he returned from his trip? What does that illustrate (see pp. 171-72)?
12. What did the master do to the servants who received a return on his money (Matt. 25:20-23; see p. 173)?
13. Why was the master upset with the servant who buried his talent (see p. 173)?
14. What warning is Christ communicating in the parable of the talents (see p. 174)?

Pondering the Principles

1. Read Isaiah 63:7-10. What do verses 7-8 say about the Lord in relation to Israel? What specifically did the Lord do for the Israelites (v. 9)? According to verse 10, what did the Israelites do, and how did the Lord respond? Scripture constantly affirms that God is patient and merciful. But as Isaiah 63:10 indicates, God's patience will eventually run out on those who rebel against Him. That truth brings up two principles worth thinking about: first, God gives everyone the opportunity to receive His mercy and love before He expresses His judgment; second, judgment is inevitable for all those who don't eventually subject themselves to God.

2. In the parable of the talents, Christ warns people to take advantage of their opportunity to enter into His kingdom. We can go a step further and state the importance of taking advantage of the little, daily opportunities we have to serve the Lord. What are some responsibilities the Lord has given you in the home, on the job, or at school? Are you satisfied with the quality of your stewardship over those things? What are one or two changes you would like to make? You might want to share your answers with a friend, and ask him those two questions as well. Then over the next few weeks, you can pray for one another and periodically check up on each other's progress. Accountability to others helps us grow toward greater Christlikeness.

12
The Tragedy of Wasted Opportunity—
Part 2

Outline

Introduction

Review
I. The Responsibility We Receive (vv. 14-15)
II. The Reaction We Have (vv. 16-18)
III. The Reckoning We Face (vv. 19-27)
　A. The Return (v. 19)

Lesson
　B. The Reckoning (vv. 20-27)
　　1. Of the faithful (vv. 20-23)
　　　a) The servant's remark
　　　　(1) His anticipation
　　　　(2) His joy
　　　b) The master's response
　　　　(1) His commendation of the faithful
　　　　(2) His generosity to the faithful
　　　　(3) His invitation to the faithful
　　　　(4) His delegation to the faithful
　　2. Of the unfaithful (vv. 24-27)
　　　a) The servant's remark (vv. 24-25)
　　　　(1) The attack
　　　　　(*a*) The reasoning
　　　　　(*b*) The reality
　　　　(2) The alibi

b) The master's response (vv. 26-27)
    (1) The unveiling of the servant's character
    (2) The unveiling of the servant's alibi
IV. The Reward We Gain (vv. 28-30)
  A. The Present Given to the Faithful
    1. The tares in the pews
    2. The transfer of the privileges
  B. The Punishment Given to the Unfaithful

Conclusion

Introduction

English poet and critic T. S. Eliot wrote a play entitled *Murder in the Cathedral*. At one point in the play the chorus portrayed the emptiness of life this way: "Yet we have gone on living, living and partly living." That line depicts the scene in Matthew 25:14-30, where we read about three servants—two are living, and one is only partly living. The latter illustrates the worthlessness of life when spiritual opportunities are wasted.

In Christ's church are both true and false servants. I'm concerned that the church isn't confronting those who don't really know the Lord. The false servants can be likened to a businessman who just opened his business and was sitting behind his desk waiting for his first client. A man walked through the door. Once the visitor was in the office, the businessman began his act. He immediately reached for the telephone, picked it up, and had a lengthy conversation with a person whom he addressed as the president of the organization. Throughout the conversation, he was giving the president advice, appearing to give wise answers. When the businessman finally hung up, he said to his visitor, "Pardon me, sir. I'm sorry to make you wait. That was the president I was just talking to. What can I do for you?" The visitor replied, "Oh, nothing. I'm just here to hook up the phone."

There are people within the church who try to look as if they are having a conversation with God, but the phone isn't hooked up. The church must not tolerate that; it's responsible to proclaim everyone's ultimate accountability to God so that the virgins without oil in their lamps or the tares that look like wheat will become convicted of their need to receive Christ. In the parable of the talents in

Matthew 25 we see a picture of the external kingdom, which is composed of true and false believers. Jesus warns that someday He will come back to separate the true from the false. And once He does that, the false will have lost their opportunity to enter into God's kingdom.

Review

I. THE RESPONSIBILITY WE RECEIVE (vv. 14-15; see pp. 166-70)

II. THE REACTION WE HAVE (vv. 16-18; see pp. 170-71)

III. THE RECKONING WE FACE (vv. 19-27)

A. The Return (v. 19; see pp. 171-72)

Lesson

B. The Reckoning (vv. 20-27)

1. Of the faithful (vv. 20-23)

a) The servant's remark

In Matthew 25:20 we read, "He that had received five talents came and brought other five talents, saying, Lord, thou deliveredst unto me five talents, behold, I have gained beside them five talents more." In the Greek text we learn that the emphasis is on the five talents, not on the servant himself.

(1) His anticipation

The servant was excited because he knew he had fulfilled his master's expectations and used his privileges well. He's one of those able to "have boldness in the day of judgment" (1 John 4:17). He won't be ashamed when the Lord returns (1 John 2:28).

179

Every believer should look forward to Christ's second coming. We should be excited about our opportunity to show Christ how we served Him while we awaited His return. We will have the joy of saying, "Lord, I received the privilege You gave me and rendered back the service You wanted."

(2) His joy

Notice the servant said, "Lord, thou deliveredst unto me five talents." He acknowledged the Lord as the source of everything. He wasn't boasting about what he had done; he knew the Lord was the source of his opportunity. The servant's statement was an exclamation of joy because he knew he had responded faithfully to the privilege.

Paul had the same kind of joy. In 2 Timothy 4:6-8 he says, "I am now ready to be offered, and the time of my departure is at hand. I have fought a good fight, I have finished my course, I have kept the faith. Henceforth there is laid up for me a crown of righteousness, which the Lord, the righteous judge, shall give me at that day." Paul was not boasting; he was sharing the fulfillment he knew from having served the Lord well. He looked forward to being with the Lord he loved.

b) The master's response

(1) His commendation of the faithful

The master recognized the integrity of his servant's heart. He knew he wasn't boasting. The master said to him, "Well done, thou good and faithful servant" (v. 21). The Greek word translated "well done" (eu) means "excellent." He was commending the servant's character, saying he was good and trustworthy.

Isn't it remarkable to think that the holy God of the universe could ever look at us and say, "Excellent, you good and faithful servant"? There is

180

nothing we could do on our own to deserve such a commendation. It's only by God's grace that we could ever be commended. We can't do anything good on our own strength; we need the power of the Holy Spirit. But what a wonderful day it will be when those who have truly served the Lord will be able to hear Him say, "Excellent, you good and trustworthy servant. You made the most of the opportunity I gave you." Such a commendation will outstrip any type of commendation we could receive here on earth. We will receive the incorruptible crown of righteousness, which the Lord gives to all them who "love his appearing" (2 Tim. 4:8)—who look forward to His return.

(2) His generosity to the faithful

The master didn't stop with commending his servant. He also said, "Thou hast been faithful over a few things, I will make thee ruler over many things" (Matt. 25:21). That shows how generous our Lord will be with us when He returns.

The kind of service you render to the Lord in eternity will be determined by the service you give to Him right now. We will all be serving Christ throughout eternity, and the rewards we receive in eternity will actually be greater opportunities for service.

When we go to heaven, we won't be sitting on a cloud playing harps for eternity. A little girl once said to me, "It sounds like heaven will be very boring." I used to wonder about that myself. Imagine playing basketball in heaven—you would get every shot! If you played golf, you would get a hole-in-one every time. That's because we would be living in absolute perfection. But heaven won't be boring. Since serving the Lord is our greatest source of joy here on earth, we will know ultimate joy in heaven because we will be serving the Lord for eternity. And based on Matthew 25:21, we know that if we are faithful with the little opportunities God gives us now, He will make us lord of many things in heaven.

Will Everyone Be Equal in Heaven?

There won't be ranks in heaven, because believers will all possess eternal life. A person can't have more or less eternal life. Believers will also be like Jesus Christ; they will be perfect, without sin. It's impossible to be any better than perfect. So we will all be equal to one another in eternity. That is confirmed by the parable of the laborers in Matthew 20. A landowner hired a number of laborers to work in his fields. Some were hired to work all day, and others were hired only an hour before the day ended. But they all received the same pay. Every Christian will receive glorification in heaven.

The only differences we will know of in heaven are the kinds of service everyone is assigned to. In the church are different levels of service requiring different types of people. The same will be true in eternity. Each believer will have differing assignments in heaven. Did you know there are different ranks among the angels (such as archangel, cherubim, and seraphim)? I believe each believer in his glorified state will have a special place of service related to that which he renders now on earth. Ultimately one's position of service in heaven depends upon God's sovereign choice (the gifts and opportunities He gives) and one's response to that choice.

Even though there will be differing levels of service in eternity, people won't sense any distinctions. No one will say, "I'm only a janitor for the left wing of such-and-such heavenly building; I'm not as important as the soloist in the choir." Each believer will be equally important. Thus, whatever service they render, it will be infinitely satisfying. The opportunity given in heaven will be in accord with God-designed capabilities. And no matter what level of responsibility believers have now, their reward will be significant.

(3) His invitation to the faithful

The servants with two and five talents received even more. Their master said, "Enter thou into the joy of thy lord" (vv. 21, 23). When Christ returns, He will invite believers to enter into His joy.

Imagine the satisfaction and joy we will have when we know redemption is accomplished, Satan is defeated, sin is abolished, the kingdom is established, and Christ will be forever glorified. We will share the Lord's joy over those things. In Hebrews 12:2 we read that "Jesus . . . for the joy that was set before him endured the cross."

(4) His delegation to the faithful

In Luke 19 is another parable giving additional insight about the rewards the Lord will give when He returns. In verse 17 a nobleman commends one of his servants, saying, "Well done, thou good servant, because thou hast been faithful in a very little, have thou authority over ten cities." In verse 19 the nobleman gives another servant authority over five cities. That tells us the servant who did the most was made ruler over the most. When the Lord sets up His kingdom on earth, He will apportion greater or lesser extents of rule according to our capacity. We will all be equal in the kingdom, but we will have distinct roles of service.

The faithful servants mentioned in Matthew 25:20-23 received a threefold commendation. They were praised, given greater responsibility, and invited to share the joy of the lord. What a glorious day it will be when we receive such commendations from our Lord!

2. Of the unfaithful (vv. 24-27)

   a) The servant's remark (vv. 24-25)

   Verses 24-25 say, "He that had received the one talent came and said, Lord, I knew thee, that thou art an hard man, reaping where thou hast not sown, and gathering where thou hast not spread, and I was afraid, and went and hid thy talent in the earth; lo, there thou hast what is thine."

That is the sad part of the parable. The servant who was given one talent represents those who profess to be believers. They say they belong to the household of God. They say their goal in life is to serve the Lord. However, two things betray such people, as illustrated by the servant in verses 24-25. First, he attacked the character of his master. That proved he didn't love and respect his master. Second, he made no use of his privileges.

(1) The attack

> The servant said to his lord, "I knew thee, that thou art an hard man" (v. 24). The phrase "I knew thee" indicates the servant was expressing an opinion. This servant doesn't represent atheists or those who hate God. He identifies himself as a servant, just as many false servants identify themselves with the church. He didn't squander his master's goods as the unjust steward in Luke 16 or spend it on riotous living as the prodigal son in Luke 15. Nor did he embezzle the money as the unmerciful servant in Matthew 18. He simply didn't do anything with his lord's money. He illustrates those who waste their spiritual opportunities. That's sad because he lived in the environment of redemption. Such people say they serve the Lord but don't. That fact will be made evident by their lack of fruit and their attack on God's character.

> The servant said his lord was "a hard man." The servant was saying, "You're unrelenting, unmerciful, and unkind. You lack compassion and sensitivity."

(a) The reasoning

> Why did he say that? Because he was full of fear. There are many people who will say to the Lord on judgment day, "Your standards

were too hard. They were too much for me. So I figured you must be an ungracious, judgmental God." They will try to give excuses for their lack of responsibility. Then at the end of verse 24 the servant accuses his master of harvesting what other people planted.

   (*b*) The reality

He certainly isn't talking about the God we know and love! How could anyone possibly characterize God as being uncompassionate and ungracious and say that He takes advantage of the benefits of other people's work? Such a person doesn't know the Lord. He pretends to, but his words betray him. The greatest joy in a Christian's life is to serve the Lord so He can benefit. Anyone who says, "I don't want to serve the Lord because He will get all the glory," doesn't understand who the Lord is. He is blind to his Master's grace, mercy, majesty, and worthiness.

(2) The alibi

To excuse himself the unfaithful servant said, "I was afraid, and went and hid thy talent in the earth; lo, there thou hast what is thine" (v. lo). The servant was saying he was afraid that if he invested the talent and lost the money, he would be punished; and that if he made a profit, it would be taken away by the master anyway. His perspective was that no matter what he did with the talent, he would lose out. He figured the best thing to do was to give the talent back when the master returned. But he was merely giving an excuse for why he wasted the privilege given to him.

b) The master's response (vv. 26-27)

(1) The unveiling of the servant's character

Matthew 25:26 says, "His lord answered and said unto him, Thou wicked and slothful servant." Notice he didn't say, "Oh, you poor man. Your theology is fouled up; you don't really understand who I am." The master knew better. He knew the servant was giving excuses. The servant knew the master wasn't ungracious or uncompassionate, just as false servants in the church know that God is full of grace and mercy. Scripture is clear about the true characteristics of God.

The master knew the servant wanted only to pursue his selfish desires. He knew the servant hid the money in the ground because it got in the way of his wickedness and lazy life-style. The servant didn't want to serve the Lord because he had no heart to do so. He made no effort to take advantage of the privilege he was given.

(2) The unveiling of the servant's alibi

After addressing the servant's wickedness and laziness, the master said, "Thou knewest that I reap where I sowed not, and gather where I have not spread?" (v. 26). The tone of the master's words are as if he were saying, "Oh, is that so? You knew that I was hard and that I expected a return?" Verse 27 continues, "Thou oughtest, therefore, to have put my money to the exchangers, and then, at my coming, I should have received mine own with interest."

If the servant really thought the master was a hard man and expected a return, then he would have given the talent to the money exchangers so it could at least earn interest. But the servant didn't do that, and the master saw through the servant's lie. The real reason the servant didn't do anything with the talent was he didn't want to bother with it. He tried to give an excuse for burying the talent, but then contradicted himself when he said he knew the master expected some type of return.

In the Roman Empire people could give their money to bankers and receive interest. The bankers loaned that money out to others, and according to historical records, charged about 12 percent interest on the loans. So people who deposited money with the bankers probably received about 6 percent interest. The Greek word translated "interest" in Matthew 25:27 is *tokos*, which means "simple interest." So the master would have probably received about 6 percent of whatever the talent was worth. That wouldn't have been like the returns on the two talents and five talents, but at least there would have been some return. It also would have been much easier to give the talent to a banker than to hide it in a hole. (Note that this parable from Jesus indicates it's permissible to invest money to get a return on it.)

The servant was unmasked as a liar. He was too lazy to do anything with the opportunity given to him.

IV. THE REWARD WE GAIN (vv. 28-30)

In verse 28 the master says, "Take, therefore, the talent from him, and give it unto him who hath ten talents." Why did he do that? Because the servant who ended up with ten talents had greater capacity.

A. The Present Given to the Faithful

1. The tares in the pews

Many people in the church today claim to serve the Lord but aren't believers. They might be ushers, teachers of children, volunteers who help maintain the church, choir members, or even pastors, elders, and deacons. They are the tares of Matthew 13:24-30. And the tares don't necessarily sit around doing nothing. Some of them are active. When I first came to Grace Church there were a couple of men on the board of elders who were not Christians. It's not uncommon for that to happen in churches today; Satan is clever. Yet from time to time, the truth about a particular false servant will be found out.

We once discovered a woman in charge of a Sunday school class at Grace Church who was taking the children to a bakery during the service. She had no interest in what was going on at the church. She thought she was serving God, and for a while it appeared she was doing so. But the truth became manifest. Some people on religious television programs purport to serve the Lord and identify with the church yet aren't really redeemed. Only God knows how many people there are who profess Christ but aren't Christians.

2. The transfer of the privileges

When the Lord returns in judgment, those who thought they were serving the Lord when they weren't will lose whatever God entrusted them with. In verse 29 Jesus says, "Unto every one that hath shall be given, and he shall have abundance; but from him that hath not shall be taken away even that which he hath." How is it possible to take something from someone who has nothing? A false servant might look like a true servant because he appears to be doing something with the spiritual privileges given to Him. But at judgment, the truth will be found out.

You may ask, "Why did the master give the one talent to the servant who had ten talents instead of the one with four talents? I don't know. Perhaps he had greater capacity for handling it. God is sovereign; He can do whatever He pleases. But the point is that God will take away privileges entrusted to false servants and give them to true servants.

B. The Punishment Given to the Unfaithful

What happened to the false servant? The master gives the answer in verse 30: "Cast the unprofitable servant into outer darkness; there shall be weeping and gnashing of teeth." The individual represented by the servant obviously is not a Christian, for he is cast into hell. The man who came to the wedding feast in Matthew 22 without a wedding garment faced the same fate. The king told his servants to "bind him hand and foot, and take him away, and cast him into outer darkness; there shall be weeping and gnashing of teeth" (v. 13). That's how hell is described in Matthew's gospel.

First John 1:5 says, "God is light, and in him is no darkness at all." Thus the absence of God is utter darkness, and hell is a place where God will never abide. The phrase "there shall be weeping and gnashing of teeth" (Matt. 25:30) depicts the unrelieved pain of being outside of God's presence.

Conclusion

In the external kingdom—the church—some are serving the Lord and are prepared for His return, and some appear to be serving Him but aren't ready for His coming. When the Lord returns, He will separate people based on the service they rendered to Him (Matt. 25:31-46). All excuses set aside, false servants will lose their spiritual privileges, which will be given to true servants to enjoy throughout eternity.

The parable of the talents is an illustration of the warning in Matthew 25:13: "Watch, therefore; for ye know neither the day nor the hour in which the Son of man cometh." You may not have to wait until the Lord returns before you face Him; if you die as an unbeliever before He returns, you will have wasted your spiritual opportunities. Whether by death or the second coming, the nature of your service will become manifest the moment you face God. It will be a fearful moment indeed for those who are caught as bridesmaids without any oil in their lamps.

Focusing on the Facts

1. Why is the servant excited in Matthew 25:20 (see p. 179)?
2. According to 1 John 2:28 and 4:17, in what way will faithful servants be able to face judgment (see p. 179)?
3. What does the faithful servant acknowledge in Matthew 25:20 (see p. 180)?

4. What commendation will the faithful receive when they see the Lord (Matt. 25:21; see p. 180)?
5. How will the Lord manifest His generosity to the faithful when He returns (see pp. 181-82)?
6. Since serving the Lord is our greatest _____ of _____ here on earth, we will know ultimate _____ in heaven because we will be serving the Lord for _____ (see p. 181).
7. Will everyone be equal in heaven? Explain (see p. 182).
8. What invitation will the Lord extend to the faithful when He returns (see pp. 182-83)?
9. What will the Lord delegate to His true servants when He returns (see p. 183)?
10. What two things betray false servants who claim their goal in life is to serve the Lord (see p. 184)?
11. What did the unfaithful servant say about his master? Does such a person really know the Lord? Explain (see p. 185).
12. What reason did the unfaithful servant give for burying the talent? What is the real reason he buried the talent (see pp. 185-86)?
13. According to Matthew 25:29, what will Christ do with the privileges He entrusted to the unfaithful (see p. 188)?
14. What is the ultimate fate of the unfaithful (Matt. 25:30; see pp. 188-89)?

Pondering the Principles

1. In Matthew 25 the servants who receive two talents and five talents both acknowledge their master as the source of the talents. Likewise, we should acknowledge that God is the source of all our privileges. He is the source of salvation, strength, wisdom, peace, blessing, and life. Does the way you use your privileges reflect your appreciation for the source of those privileges? Make a habit of thanking the Lord for the privileges He has given you.

2. In our society the phrase "thank you" is uncommon. Some people have gradually eliminated it from their vocabulary, and many of those who still use it say it without sincerity. As a Christian, thankfulness is to be part of your character. Your thankfulness can be a testimony to Christ in a world filled with ingratitude. Do you say thank you to others around you as of-

ten as you should? What are some other ways to show thankfulness besides saying thank you? Get together with your family or a friend: discuss what you have to be thankful for and why it's good to express thanks. Be ready for some new insights!

13
The Judgment of the Nations—Part 1

Outline

Introduction
A. The Truth About Judgment
    1. The inevitability of judgment
    2. The indemnity from judgment
    3. The impartation of judgment
B. The Truth About Jesus
    1. The revealing of the King
    2. The rejection of the King
    3. The return of the King

Lesson
  I. The Judge
    A. The Word from the Son of Man
    B. The Wait for the Son of Man
    C. The Work of the Son of Man
      1. At His first coming
      2. At His second coming
        a) With the angels
        b) With the saints
  II. The Time of Judgment
 III. The Place of Judgment
 IV. The Subjects of Judgment

Introduction

The text we will be studying in the next few lessons is Matthew 25:31-46, which talks about judgment. In this lesson we'll be looking specifically at verses 31-32, which say, "When the Son of man shall come in glory, and all the holy angels with him, then shall he sit upon the throne of his glory. And before him shall be gathered all the nations; and he shall separate them one from another, as a shepherd divideth his sheep from the goats."

A. The Truth About Judgment

1. The inevitability of judgment

Numbers 32:23 says, "Be sure your sin will find you out." There is no way to escape sin. It must be punished. God stands in the place of a holy Judge who must execute punishment. Psalm 90:8 says, "Thou hast set our iniquities before thee, our secret sins in the light of thy countenance." What might appear secret to us is in full view of God's eyes. In Proverbs we read, "Evil pursueth sinners" (13:21). The consequence of sin is like one's shadow; it cannot be removed. Isaiah 3:11 says, "Woe unto the wicked! It shall be ill with him; for the reward of his hands shall be given him."

Judgment for sin is inevitable. Romans 1:18 says "the wrath of God is revealed from heaven against *all* ungodliness and unrighteousness of men" (emphasis added). Romans 2:9 adds, "Tribulation and anguish, upon every soul of man that doeth evil."

2. The indemnity from judgment

Will Christians face the judgment of God? No. They have the marvelous privilege of having their substitute—Jesus Christ—take their punishment. By God's grace, when you put your faith in Christ, your sins are judged in Christ. That's why Christ died on the cross. He paid the penalty for all the sin in this world. Those who receive Christ have the debt of sin paid for. However, those who do not accept Christ's lordship and His atonement for sin will bear the punishment for their own sin.

3. The impartation of judgment

Adam sinned, and the world fell under a curse. One sin committed by one man devastated the entire human race. That shows how God feels about sin. In Genesis 6, when God saw the utter wickedness of the people on the earth, He drowned every man with the exception of eight righteous people. Throughout the Bible we read of various cities and individuals that have been destroyed in judgment. Those are warnings that God judges sin. Hebrews 9:27 says, "It is appointed unto men once to die, but after this the judgment." Anyone who believes that good works or God's kindness—apart from salvation through Christ—will make God overlook sin is wrong.

Judgment is imminent. And in Matthew 25:31-46, we will be taking a close look at the judgment that will take place at Christ's second coming.

B. The Truth About Jesus

1. The revealing of the King

Matthew presents Christ as King. In chapter 1 he traces Jesus' royal lineage. In chapter 2 He shows that the current ruler, Herod, felt threatened by the birth of Christ. It was Matthew who spoke of the wise men—the oriental kingmakers—who offered Jesus homage and presented Him royal gifts. In chapter 3 He writes of Christ's herald, John the Baptist, who was appointed to announce His coming. In chapter 4 he notes that when Satan offered Christ all the kingdoms of the world, Christ rejected the offer because He knew He was entitled to rule the world. Christ's kingship is revealed again in the Sermon on the Mount, which presents the standards of Christ's kingdom. Then Matthew writes about Christ's miracles to show His absolute sovereignty and power. In Matthew 28:18 he concludes his gospel with Christ's saying, "All authority is given unto me in heaven and in earth."

2. The rejection of the King

Sadly, Matthew also speaks of the rejection of Christ. Not long after the angelic host heralded Christ's birth, many mothers were weeping because Herod slaughtered their babies in an attempt to kill the baby Jesus

(Matt. 2:16-18). Joseph and Mary fled to Egypt to protect their baby's life. When they returned to their homeland, they lived in obscurity in the nondescript village of Nazareth. He grew up there as a prophet without honor (Matt. 13:57). In fact, some people in Nazareth even tried to throw Him off a cliff (Luke 4:28-30).

Matthew says in his gospel that Christ's herald (John the Baptist) was beheaded (Matt. 14:10). The religious leaders accused Jesus of being a glutton and drunkard (Matt. 11:19) and said He was of Satan (Matt. 12:24). In a parable in chapter 22, Christ speaks of the rejection He faced and says the Jewish leaders want to kill Him just as they had killed all the other prophets of God. When Christ died, He said to the Father, "My God, my God, why hast thou forsaken me?" (Matt. 27:46).

3. The return of the King

Matthew goes into the greatest detail about Christ's second coming in Matthew 24-25. There are other references to the Lord's return in Matthew as well: Matthew 16:27-28 says, "The Son of man shall come in the glory of his Father with his angels, and then he shall reward every man according to his works. Verily I say unto you, There are some standing here, who shall not taste of death, till they see the Son of man coming in his kingdom." Matthew 19:28 speaks of the regeneration, which is when Christ will sit on the throne of His glory and the disciples will sit on twelve thrones judging the twelve tribes of Israel.

Matthew 25:31 says that when the Son of Man comes, He will sit on His throne. Immediately after that (v. 34) He begins the judgment process (see pp. 70-71). It is uncertain when the judgment will take place in relation to the end of the Tribulation. The second half of the Tribulation will last for three-and-a-half years (1,260 days; Rev. 11:3). But Daniel said that 1,335 days will pass before the kingdom is completely established, which gives us seventy-five days after the end of the Tribulation. What will happen during those seventy-five days? We don't know; but it is certain that Christ will come in judgment during that time. If judgment takes place at the beginning of the seventy-five days, it could be that the remaining days are a period of cleaning up after judgment. It may be that the dead bodies from the terrible battle of Armageddon will be buried during that time (Ezek. 39:12-13).

Regardless of exactly what will happen, we know that once Christ returns, there will be no time for unsaved people to suddenly receive Christ. It will be too late. Judgment will take place immediately, just as it does the moment a person dies. The minute you die, the decision you made regarding Christ is crystallized for eternity. There will be no further opportunity for unregenerate people to make a choice.

Lesson

I. THE JUDGE

A. The Word from the Son of Man

John 5:22 says, "The Father judgeth no man, but hath committed all judgment unto the Son." In Matthew 28 Christ says, "All authority is given unto me in heaven and in earth" (v. 18). So the Father has delegated judgment to the Son. Matthew 25:31-32 says, "When the Son of man shall come in his glory, and all the holy angels with him, then shall he sit upon the throne of his glory. And before him shall be gathered all the nations; and he shall separate them one from another." "The Son of man" in Matthew 25 is none other than the Lord Jesus Christ.

Why Did Christ Call Himself "the Son of Man"?

The title Jesus used most often for Himself is "the Son of man." I believe there are several reasons for that.

1. It confirmed His humiliation

By calling Himself the Son of Man, Jesus affirmed He was God incarnate—God become man. It was an affirmation of the ser-

197

vant spirit He had. Matthew 20:28 says, "The Son of man came not to be ministered unto, but to minister, and to give his life a ransom for many." The phrase "Son of man" emphasizes Christ's condescension and His identification with us.

2. It was less offensive to His enemies

If Christ had called Himself "the Son of God" and not "the Son of man," He might have generated hostility. The Jewish religious leaders would have been especially resentful of that. Even with circumstances as they were, the Jewish leaders took His life after three years of ministry. God had already preordained the time of Christ's death, and He controlled the circumstances that led up to it. That Christ didn't call Himself "Son of God" in Matthew 25:31 to keep from being offensive is only conjecture, but that may explain to us why He didn't.

3. It was more subtle than other titles

Had Christ called Himself "Son of God" or even "King" all the time, His friends would have probably put greater pressure on Him to establish His rule immediately. They would have wanted Him to end the Roman rule over Israel. Jesus wanted to keep a low profile in line with the purpose of His first coming.

4. It provided a contrast with His future role

In Matthew 25:31 Christ calls Himself the Son of Man, but then in verses 34 and 40 He calls Himself the King, because He will establish His rule when He returns. He uses both titles for Himself in Matthew 25 to show that the Son of Man and the King are the same. When He speaks of future judgment, He calls Himself King to show the transition from His humiliation to His glorification.

Christ didn't flaunt His kingship at His first coming. In Matthew 24-25, He is speaking privately to the disciples, not publicly before a crowd. Later on when Pilate asked Jesus if He was a king, Jesus responded indirectly (John 18:37). Even though Jesus didn't aggressively assert that He was King, the people knew He claimed to be so. The sign posted on His cross said, "Jesus of Nazareth, the King of the Jews" (John 19:19). So Christ downplayed His kingship at His first coming and called Himself the Son of Man.

B. The Wait for the Son of Man

When Christ returns, He will judge the world. Unbelievers may be enjoying themselves now, but when the Lord returns their party will end. The world is rapidly accelerating toward its doom.

The promise of Christ's returning to judge the world is not isolated in Matthew. Jude 14-15 says, "Enoch also, the seventh from Adam, prophesied . . . saying, Behold, the Lord cometh with ten thousands of his saints, to execute judgment upon all, and to convict all that are ungodly." Enoch probably declared the first prophecy of Christ's second coming, and that was back in the earliest period of the Old Testament era.

C. The Work of the Son of Man

1. At His first coming

What's remarkable about Christ is not that He will return but that He came at all the first time to make forgiveness possible for man. God, being infinitely holy, could have come to earth the first time to judge man for his sinfulness. Instead, He came to redeem us. He showed love to us when we were unlovely. He wanted to offer us salvation. He became a servant and died on a cross so that we might live. He has yet to judge man. He will do that later. But when He does, it will be a terrible judgment that will surely be beyond anything we can envision or communicate.

2. At His second coming

a) With the angels

Matthew 25:31 says that when Christ returns, angels will be with Him. Paul writes in 2 Thessalonians 1:7, "The Lord Jesus shall be revealed from heaven with his mighty angels." Imagine what the scene will be like to those on the earth at that time. Matthew 24:29-30 says, "Immediately after the tribulation of those days shall the sun be darkened, and the moon shall not give its light, and the stars shall fall from heaven, and the powers of the heavens shall be shaken. And then shall appear the sign of the Son of man in heaven; and then shall all the tribes of the earth mourn, and they shall see the Son of man coming in the clouds of heaven with power and great glory."

After the heavens become dark, Christ will return in full blazing glory. The light will be so blinding that the unregenerate people of the world will cry for the rocks and the mountains to fall on them to hide them from the coming wrath. They won't be able to stand Christ's unveiled glory. Those who do not know God will be punished with everlasting destruction, and those who are believers will glorify Christ.

b) With the saints

Colossians 3:4 says, "When Christ, who is our life, shall appear, then shall ye also appear with him in glory." The saints who were raptured at the beginning of the Tribulation as well as the spirits of the Old Testament saints will return with Christ to establish His kingdom.

Revelation 19 describes that scene for us in great detail. In verse 11 John says, "I saw heaven opened and, behold, a white horse; and he that sat upon him was called Faithful and True, and in righteousness he doth judge and make war." That's the second time John saw heaven open up. The first time was in Revelation 4:1. I believe the first time he saw it opened up was to bring in the raptured church, and the second time was to let Christ return with the saints.

Christ will come as a conquering King on a white horse. The white horse symbolizes His holiness. Verses 12-14 say, "His eyes were like a flame of fire, and on his head were many crowns; and he had a name written, that no man knew, but he himself. And he was clothed with a vesture dipped in blood; and his name is called The Word of God. And the armies that were in heaven followed him upon white horses, clothed in fine linen, white and clean." The angels and the saints compose the army that will return with Christ.

Verses 15-16 continue, "Out of his mouth goeth a sharp sword, that with it he should smite the nations, and he shall rule them with a rod of iron; and he treadeth the winepress of the fierceness and wrath of Almighty God. And he hath on his vesture and on his thigh a name written, King of kings, and Lord of lords." When Christ returns, judgment will be immediate. There will be no time to change your mind about Him.

II. THE TIME OF JUDGMENT

Matthew 25:31-32 says judgment will take place when the Son of Man returns. Yet we don't know exactly when He will return once the Tribulation ends. What we do know is that when Christ returns, He will come with all the holy angels and His saints. He will come in full glory and will "sit upon the throne of his glory" (v. 31). Then comes judgment. Verse 32 says, "Before him shall be gathered all the nations; and he shall separate them one from another, as a shepherd divideth his sheep from the goats." So men will either be judged at the moment of their death or at the moment of Christ's return.

III. THE PLACE OF JUDGMENT

Matthew 25:31 says Christ will "sit upon the throne of his glory." Where is that throne? The answer is in Isaiah 9:6-7, a prophecy about the coming King: "His name shall be called Wonderful, Counselor, The Mighty God, The Everlasting Father, The Prince of Peace. Of the increase of his government and peace there shall be no end, upon the throne of David, and upon his kingdom, to order it, and to establish it with justice and with righteousness from henceforth even forever." Christ will judge from the throne of David, which is on Mount Zion in the city of Jerusalem (Heb. 12:22). An angel says this about Jesus in Luke 1:32-33: "He shall be great, and shall be called the Son of the Highest; and the Lord God shall give unto him the throne of his father, David. And he shall reign over the house of Jacob forever; and of his kingdom there shall be no end." Christ will rule on the throne of Jacob in Jerusalem.

That will become a historical reality in an actual geographical location.

Zechariah 14:4 says that when Christ returns, "His feet shall stand in that day upon the Mount of Olives, which is before Jerusalem on the east, and the Mount of Olives shall cleave in its midst toward the east and toward the west, and there shall be a very great valley; and half of the mountain shall remove toward the north, and half of it toward the south." When Mount Zion is split to create the new valley, the topography of Jerusalem as we know it now will be destroyed. Why will that valley be created? The prophet Joel says this: "Assemble yourselves, and come, all ye nations, and gather yourselves together round about; there cause thy mighty ones to come down, O Lord. Let the nations be wakened, and come up to the Valley of Jehoshaphat; for there will I sit to judge all the nations round about. Put in the sickle; for the harvest is ripe; come, get down; for the press is full, the vats overflow; for their wickedness is great. Multitudes, multitudes in the valley of decision; for the day of the Lord is near in the valley of decision" (Joel 3:11-14).

The valley created at Christ's return will be the valley of decision—the place where God determines the eternal destiny of those on earth at the time. Verses 15-17 continue, "The sun and the moon shall be darkened, and the stars shall withdraw their shining. The Lord also shall roar out of Zion, and utter his voice from Jerusalem, and the heavens and the earth shall shake; but the Lord will be the hope of his people, and the strength of the children of Israel. So shall ye know that I am the Lord, your God, dwelling in Zion, my holy mountain; then shall Jerusalem be holy, and there shall no strangers pass through her any more." The Lord will instantly sanctify the city. And He will soon return bodily to reign there.

IV. THE SUBJECTS OF JUDGMENT

Matthew 25:32 says that when Christ returns all the nations will be gathered before Him. The word translated "nations" is the Greek word *ethna,* which means "all the people"—everyone alive at the time of the second coming. They will be gathered before the Lord, and "He shall separate them one from another, as a shepherd divideth his sheep from the goats" (v. 32).

Who will be alive at the second coming of Christ? We know they weren't redeemed at the time the Tribulation began because they didn't go with the church at the rapture. But during the Tribulation, 144,000 Jewish believers (Rev. 7:4-8) and two special witnesses (Rev. 11:3-12) will preach the gospel all over the world. There will also be an angel preaching the gospel message "to every nation, and kindred, and tongue, and people" (Rev. 14:6). Many people will be saved as a result. Revelation 7:9 says a great multitude of Gentiles will be saved, and Romans 11:26 says "all Israel shall be saved."

There will also be many unsaved people alive at the time of Christ's return. Many unsaved people will be killed during the Tribulation as God pours out His wrath, but those who survive will face Christ in judgment. By that time, it will be too late for them to make a decision to receive Christ. Matthew 25:46 says that when Christ returns, He shall send the ungodly into everlasting punishment and the righteous into eternal life. There will be no second chance.

Focusing on the Facts

1. What does God say about man's sin? Support your answer (see p. 194).
2. Will Christians face judgment? Explain (see p. 194).
3. What do John 5:22 and Matthew 28:18 confirm for us (see p. 197)?
4. What are some likely reasons that Christ called Himself the Son of Man (see pp. 197-98)?
5. What remarkable truth should we appreciate about Christ in relation to His first and second comings (see p. 199)?
6. With whom will Christ return according to 2 Thessalonians 1:7? Describe the scene from the perspective of those alive on the earth at that time (see pp. 199-200).
7. How does Revelation 19:11-16 describe Christ's return? Who will be with Him when He returns (see pp. 200-201)?
8. Where will Christ sit when He comes in judgment (Matt. 25:31; Heb. 12:22; see p. 201)?
9. How do Zechariah 14:4 and Joel 3:11-17 describe Christ's return (see p. 203)?
10. Who will be alive at the second coming of Christ (see p. 203)?

Pondering the Principles

1. Reread the section entitled "Why Did Christ Call Himself the Son of Man?" on pages 197-98. Imagine the transition Christ made in leaving His glorious place in heaven to become a servant on earth. What did He have to give up? If an earthly king did the same thing, how long do you think he could tolerate it? What does the fact that Christ was willing to humble Himself tell you about Him? Spend some time now thanking Him for all that He went through to make your salvation possible.

2. Read Revelation 19:11-16 and Joel 3:11-17, considering the power, majesty, and glory that will be displayed when Christ returns. God is mighty, and believers will witness the fullness of all that He is when they enter into His eternal kingdom. Meditate on Psalm 96, and let your heart respond in praise to God as you reflect on His majesty.

14
The Judgment of the Nations—Part 2

Outline

Introduction

Review
I. The Judge
II. The Time of Judgment
III. The Place of Judgment
IV. The Subjects of Judgment

Lesson
A. What Will Happen to Those on Earth at Christ's Return?
B. What About Believers Who Aren't on Earth at Christ's Return?
  1. Some will be taken up before the Tribulation
    a) The rapture of the church
    b) The renewal of dead believers
  2. Some will be taken up during the Tribulation
  3. Some will be taken up after the Tribulation
C. What About Believers Who Are on Earth at Christ's Return?

I. A Literal Kingdom Is the Only Adequate Confirmation of God's Promises
II. A Literal Kingdom Is Consistent with Christ's Teaching About the End Times
III. A Literal Kingdom Is the Only Logical Interpretation of Messianic Prophecy

IV. A Literal Kingdom Is the Best Way for Christ to Show His Kingship

V. A Literal Kingdom Is the Only Way to Bridge Human History to Eternal Glory

Introduction

Jesus' disciples knew that one day the Messiah would establish a glorious, visible kingdom on earth—that the world would be the way God wanted it to be. They looked forward to the fulfillment of Malachi 1:11, which says, "From the rising of the sun even unto the going down of the same, my name shall be great among the nations, and in every place incense shall be offered unto my name, and a pure offering; for my name shall be great among the nations, saith the Lord of hosts." Ezekiel also talked about God's future kingdom on earth (Ezek. 40-48). He wrote of the glorious new Temple that would be built, the priests that would make offerings, and the celebrations that would be observed. That Temple will not have the Ark of the Covenant to represent God's presence, as God Himself will be present in the Temple. The disciples became excited when Jesus taught them about His kingdom and asked, "When shall these things be? And what shall be the sign of thy coming, and of the end of the age?" (Matt. 24:3). Jesus answers those questions in Matthew 24-25, and in this lesson we will be studying about the judgment that will take place when Christ returns.

Review

I. THE JUDGE (see pp. 197-201)

II. THE TIME OF JUDGMENT (see p. 201)

III. THE PLACE OF JUDGMENT (see p. 201-3)

IV. THE SUBJECTS OF JUDGMENT

Lesson

A. What Will Happen to Those on Earth at Christ's Return?

When Christ returns, there will be people alive on earth. They will be the survivors of the Tribulation. Some will be saved, and others will not. Matthew 25:32 says, "Before him shall be gathered all the nations; and he shall separate them one from another, as a shepherd divideth his sheep from the goats." All the people will be separated into one of two categories: the sheep (Christians) or the goats (non-Christians). From there they will go on to their eternal destiny. The sheep will go to heaven, and the goats will go to hell. The category they go into will be determined by their relationship to Christ and nothing else. No distinction will be made between Jew or Gentile.

B. What About Believers Who Aren't on Earth at Christ's Return?

1. Some will be taken up before the Tribulation

   a) The rapture of the church

   Right now we are living in the church age. God is gathering all the people who will be a part of the Body of Christ. When the fullness of the church age has come, the church will be taken out of the world (1 Thess. 4:17). If Christ were to call us right now, every believer would be taken up into heaven. And on the way up there, the believer's lowly body will be transformed into a glorious body like that of the Lord Jesus Christ (Phil. 3:21).

   b) The renewal of dead believers

   What about Christians who have already died? First Thessalonians 4:16 says, "The dead in Christ shall rise first." When Christ calls us at the rapture, the dead will rise and those of us who are alive will join them. But where do the spirits of dead Christians reside while we await the rapture? When believers die, their spirits go to be with the Lord (2 Cor. 5:8). When the rapture occurs, they will receive new, glorified bodies. It won't matter if their old bodies are long gone—God will create their new bodies out of nothing.

When a Christian dies, his spirit goes to heaven, and his body stays on earth. He doesn't need his body because God is Spirit (John 4:24), and the believer's spirit can communicate with God. When you communicate, your spirit—not your physical body—is involved. The spirit is your real self, and it simply resides in a physical body. Nevertheless the Lord promises this in 1 Corinthians 15:52: "In the twinkling of an eye, at the last trump; for the trumpet shall sound, and the dead shall be raised incorruptible, and we shall be changed." The new bodies that rise from the grave will be joined with their spirits at the rapture, and those of us who are alive at the rapture will be changed as we ascend. Our bodies will no longer be debilitated by sin.

The new bodies we have will be fit for both heaven and earth. When Jesus rose from the grave, He ate, walked, and talked with His disciples (e.g., Luke 24:33-43). Later He ascended into heaven (Acts 1:9) to sit down at the right hand of God's throne (Heb. 10:12). That we will have bodies fit for earth and heaven helps prove that Christ's future kingdom on earth will be literal and visible. Why would God bother restoring the earth in eternity (Rev. 21:1) if He weren't going to give us bodies that could live on it?

Those who became believers before the Tribulation—whether dead or alive—will be taken up in the rapture. They will be given glorified bodies and take part in the marriage supper of the Lamb (Rev. 19:9). It will be a time of receiving rewards (1 Cor. 3:12-15; 2 Tim. 4:8) and enjoying our new, transformed bodies.

2. Some will be taken up during the Tribulation

While the church is in heaven, the world will be going through the Tribulation. The Antichrist will be running rampant all over the earth. Demons will be let loose from hell, and Satan will be cast down from heaven. Together they will wreak havoc on earth. Because the church is gone from the earth, evil will not be restrained. Sin will be allowed to run its full course during those seven years before God brings judgment. Nevertheless many people will become saved during the Tribulation (Rom. 11:26; Rev. 7:9).

3. Some will be taken up after the Tribulation

One question that isn't dealt with in the rapture is, When will the Old Testament saints be resurrected? The bodies of the Old Testament saints are still here on earth, but their spirits are in heaven. I believe Jesus took them to heaven after He died (Eph. 4:8-10). When Christ died, His spirit went to a place of blessedness (cf. Luke 16:22) where all the souls of the Old Testament saints were and carried them to glory. But the bodies of the Old Testament saints will have to wait until after the Tribulation before they are resurrected and glorified. They will be resurrected when the bodies of the Tribulation saints are resurrected.

The Tribulation is like an addendum to the Old Testament era, because the church age comes to an end once the Tribulation begins. In Daniel, the Tribulation is the seventieth week in his seventy-week prophecy (9:26-27). The church age is the unforeseen period between the sixty-ninth and seventieth weeks. The Lord did His work through the nation Israel before the church age and will do so again after the church age. Thus the bodies of the Old Testament saints will be resurrected at the same time as the bodies of the Tribulation saints. So the only people resurrected at the rapture are those who became saved during the church age.

Daniel 12:1-2 confirms that there will be a great resurrection after the Tribulation: "At that time shall Michael stand up, the great prince who standeth for the children of thy people [Israel], and there shall be a time of trouble . . . and at that time thy people shall be delivered, every one that shall be found written in the book. And many of those who sleep in the dust of the earth shall awake, some to everlasting life."

In our glorified bodies, we—like angels—will be able to go wherever we wish. Our bodies will be fit for both earth and heaven. We will be able to ascend to or descend from the new city of Jerusalem, which will hover above the earth (Rev. 21:2).

C. What About Believers Who Are on Earth at Christ's Return?

Believers who survive the Tribulation will be brought into the kingdom in their earthly bodies. There will be no change for them. They are the ones who will bear children in Christ's earthly kingdom (Isa. 11:8; 65:20). And those children will bear the offspring who rebel against Christ at the end of the millennial kingdom (Rev. 20:7-9).

Some people wonder how anyone could possibly rebel against Christ after witnessing His reign and power. But look at the rejection Christ faced the first time He came to earth. That people will still reject Christ even when they see Him rule in perfect wisdom, love, and power illustrates the depravity of unregenerate people.

The millennial kingdom Christ establishes will be indwelt by both glorified and unglorified believers. Those who are glorified will know life in both heaven and earth, and those who remain unglorified will live only on earth. The unglorified believers will still eat meals, plant crops, cook, and work. The glorified and unglorified will mingle together. Christ, after He was glorified, still mingled with His disciples (Luke 24:33-43), and Abraham and Sarah dined with angels (Gen. 18:1-10).

Will the one-thousand-year reign of Christ be a literal, earthly kingdom? Those who are amillennialists say there won't be an actual, physical kingdom on earth. They believe the Bible's teachings about Christ's future rule refers to a spiritual kingdom in our hearts. Yet the Bible indicates Christ's rule will be a literal one. For example,

1 Corinthians 15 says we will receive glorified bodies at the rapture. What is the sense of God's giving us glorified bodies if there is no physical kingdom on earth? Amillennialists often say belief in a literal, earthly kingdom is recent. However, according to German theologian Erich Sauer in his *The Triumph of the Crucified* (Grand Rapids: Eerdmans, 1953), such belief goes back to the first century. Early writers such as Papias, Justin, Tertullian, and Hippolytus affirmed the church's convictions about a future, earthly kingdom. Sauer says that with the growth of Catholicism, millennialism was pushed aside (p. 144). Revelation 20:4 clearly states believers will reign with Christ for a literal one-thousand-year period.

A person who denies that Christ will set up a physical kingdom on earth and reign from Jerusalem must do three things. First he has to say that all God's prophetic promises to the rebellious nation of Israel apply only to the church, defined as a spiritual Israel. That means God's promises that were supposed to be fulfilled in a literal sense will only be fulfilled in a spiritual sense. Second, he must say that the prophecies about the kingdom have already been fulfilled or that they are being fulfilled now. Third, he must spiritualize Old Testament prophecies that relate to an actual place or event. However the Bible says that Christ will come again, just as He came two thousand years ago. Let's look at the evidence for a literal kingdom, much of which comes from Erich Sauer's insights on the issue (pp. 144-53).

I. A LITERAL KINGDOM IS THE ONLY ADEQUATE CONFIRMATION OF GOD'S PROMISES

God said He was going to bring a kingdom of peace ruled by the Messiah (Isa. 9:6-7). If He doesn't fulfill that prophecy, then we can question His faithfulness. But Romans 11:29 confirms that we can trust God: "The gifts and calling of God are without repentance." In context that verse is referring to Israel. God's promises to Israel will never change. God's promise to Abraham in Genesis 12:1-3 about blessing Israel as a nation was unconditional. It wasn't dependent on Israel's obedience to God's law (Rom. 4:13-14). God says He will keep that promise for the sake of His truthfulness and even for Abraham's sake (Gen. 26:24).

Jeremiah 31:35-36 specifically says, "Thus saith the Lord, who giveth the sun for a light by day, and the ordinances of the moon and of the stars for a light by night, who divideth the sea

when its waves roar; the Lord of hosts is his name: If those ordinances depart from before me, saith the Lord, then the seed
of Israel also shall cease from being a nation before me forever." God will not change His promise to Israel. To spiritualize those promises away and say that the church is Israel is to
say God is unfaithful.

II. A LITERAL KINGDOM IS CONSISTENT WITH CHRIST'S TEACHING ABOUT THE END TIMES

In Matthew 23:37-39 Jesus says, "O Jerusalem, Jerusalem, thou
that killest the prophets, and stonest them who are sent unto
thee, how often would I have gathered thy children together,
even as a hen gathereth her chickens under her wings, and ye
would not! Behold, your house is left unto you desolate. For I
say unto you, Ye shall not see me henceforth, till ye shall say,
Blessed is he that cometh in the name of the Lord." That indicates there *will* come a day when Israel receives her Messiah.

Jesus says to His disciples in Matthew 19:28, "Verily I say unto
you that ye who have followed me, in the regeneration, when
the Son of man shall sit on the throne of his glory, ye also shall
sit upon twelve thrones, judging the twelve tribes of Israel."
That is a literal prophecy; Jesus was saying the disciples will
rule in His kingdom. So to deny a literal kingdom is to deny
what Christ taught about His kingdom.

III. A LITERAL KINGDOM IS THE ONLY LOGICAL INTERPRE-TATION OF MESSIANIC PROPHECY

If you don't allow for a literal earthly kingdom, then there's no
way to logically interpret Old Testament prophecy. There are
more than three hundred prophecies about the Messiah in the
Old Testament. For example, Micah 5:2 says Christ would be
from Bethlehem. Is there a secret spiritual interpretation for
that? No; Christ's birth in Bethlehem is a historical reality
(Matt. 2:1). Zechariah 9:9 says Christ would enter Jerusalem on
a donkey. That really happened; Jesus rode into Jerusalem on
the last week of His earthly life on a donkey (Matt. 21:1-9). Isaiah 53:8-9, 12 says He would die for the sins of the world and
be buried in a rich man's tomb; Psalm 16:10 says He would rise
on the third day. All those things really happened; they cannot
be disputed.

If all the prophecies about Christ's first coming were literal, how can we say the prophecies of His second coming won't be literal? How can we say Christ won't really come down to the Mount of Olives and split it to create a valley (Zech. 14:4) and that He won't really rule for a thousand years on earth (Rev. 20:4)? The Bible doesn't say anything about the church's replacing Israel. If God says He will reestablish His people Israel, then He will.

IV. A LITERAL KINGDOM IS THE BEST WAY FOR CHRIST TO SHOW HIS KINGSHIP

If the earth is destroyed someday and there is no new physical earth (Rev. 21:1), then how will Christ show He is truly the ruler of this world? When will He be able to show what could have been done with creation?

There will be unbelievers in Christ's future kingdom. At the end of Christ's one-thousand-year earthly reign, the unbelievers will join sides with Satan, who will have just been released, and rebel against Christ's rule (Rev. 20:7-9). How could they rebel unless they could see Christ's rule in a physical sense? Their defeat will be an eternal testimony to all the beings of heaven and earth that Christ is the supreme King who can bring the diversity of His creation into harmony, even when sin does exist.

V. A LITERAL KINGDOM IS THE ONLY WAY TO BRIDGE HUMAN HISTORY TO ETERNAL GLORY

The kingdom of Christ on earth is the bridge to eternity. First Corinthians 15:24-25 says, "Then cometh the end, when he [Christ] shall have delivered up the kingdom to God, even the Father, when he shall have put down all rule and all authority and power. For he must reign, till he hath put all enemies under his feet." At the time of His coming, Christ will put down all human rule and establish His kingdom. At its end He will put down a rebellion (Rev. 20:7-10) and then usher in the eternal state.

Since the time the earth fell under the curse of sin, God has wanted to redeem the earth and have it presented to Him. That's what Christ will do during the millennial kingdom: He will change things through His rule and destroy all His enemies. First Corinthians 15:28 says, "When all things shall be subdued unto him, then shall the Son also himself be subject unto him that put all things under him, that God may be all in all." During the millennial kingdom the Lord will take back, restore, and regenerate the earth to make it fit to offer to God. That process will begin during the Tribulation when Christ is handed the title deed to the earth, and He opens it up seal by seal to purify the earth and bring it under His control (Rev. 5-11). At the end of Christ's one-thousand-year rule, Satan will be let loose a little while to deceive people and attempt a final uprising against the Lord. Christ will then destroy all the ungodly and offer up the kingdom to God. And in that eternal kingdom, the righteous will "shine forth as the sun in the kingdom of their Father" (Matt. 13:43).

Focusing on the Facts

1. The disciples looked forward to the fulfillment of what Old Testament prophecies (see p. 206)?
2. What will happen to the people alive on earth when Christ returns (see p. 207)?
3. What will determine whether a person goes to heaven or hell (see p. 207)?
4. What is God doing now during the church age? What does He plan to do at the end of the church age, according to 1 Thessalonians 4:17 (see p. 207)?
5. When the rapture takes place, what will happen to Christians who have already died (1 Thess. 4:16; see p. 207)?
6. What does 2 Corinthians 5:8 say happens when a believer dies? What promise does 1 Corinthians 15:52 make regarding those Christians who have already died (see pp. 207-8)?
7. Will people be saved during the Tribulation? Use Scripture to support your answer (see p. 209).
8. If the Old Testament saints aren't resurrected at the rapture, when will they be resurrected? Explain (see p. 209).
9. Believers who are alive on earth at the time of Christ's return will enter the kingdom in their earthly bodies, not in glorified bodies. What evidence in Scripture verifies that (see p. 210)?
10. What illustrations in Scripture show us that glorified and unglorified believers will be able to mingle in Christ's earthly kingdom (see p. 210)?

11. What do amillennialists say about the one-thousand-year reign of Christ (see p. 210)?
12. What three things must a person do who denies that Christ will set up a physical kingdom on earth (see p. 211)?
13. Why is a literal millennial kingdom the only adequate confirmation of God's promises (see pp. 211-12)?
14. How does Christ's teaching about the end times confirm a literal, earthly millennial kingdom (see p. 212)?
15. What are some examples of messianic prophecy regarding Christ's first coming? How were those prophecies fulfilled, and what does that tell us about messianic prophecies regarding the second coming (see pp. 212-13)?
16. Explain how a literal, earthly one-thousand-year kingdom would function as a bridge from human history to eternal glory (see pp. 213-14).

Pondering the Principles

1. One of the most beautiful promises Christ made to His followers is in John 14:3. He said He is preparing a place right now for us in heaven. At the rapture, He will call us and take us home to be where He is. Memorize that verse, letting it remind you of your importance to Christ and the certainty that you will be with Him personally someday: "If I go and prepare a place for you, I will come again, and receive you to Myself; that where I am, there you may be also" (NASB).

2. Reread the section explaining why Christ will rule a literal, visible, millennial kingdom on earth (see pp. 211-14). Using the material in that section, write out a brief reply you might give to an amillennialist should one happen to ask you what you think about Christ's millennial kingdom.

15
The Judgment of the Nations—Part 3

Outline

Introduction
A. Temporal Judgment
B. Eternal Judgment

Review
 I. The Judge
 II. The Time of Judgment
 III. The Place of Judgment
 IV. The Subjects of Judgment

Lesson
 V. The Process of Judgment
   A. The Separation
   B. The Sentencing
     1. Of the righteous
       a) The invitation
         (1) It's based on God's blessing
         (2) It's based on an inheritance
         (3) It's based on God's plan
       b) The inquiry
       c) The illustration
     2. Of the unrighteous
       a) The command
       b) The claim
       c) The confrontation
       d) The condemnation

Conclusion

Introduction

The Bible has much to say about judgment. Psalm 7:11 says, "God is angry with the wicked every day." Psalm 1:5 says, "The ungodly shall not stand in the judgment." The reason the Bible speaks frequently of judgment is because God is continually concerned about dealing with sin.

Many people think that references to judgment in the Bible are largely restricted to the Old Testament. People say, "In the Old Testament God was always judging people and destroying whole nations. And in the New Testament, God is presented as a God of love." However, the message of judgment is equally prominent in the New Testament. God is also presented as a God of love in the Old Testament. The only real difference in the way the Old and New Testaments present God as judge is in the nature of the judgment He imparted.

A. Temporal Judgment

The judgments of the Old Testament generally have to do with temporal judgment on earth. When God imparted judgment in the Old Testament, it was to destroy a nation or to punish a person. That emphasizes that God will raise up and put down certain people or nations. It's true that temporal judgment appears in the New Testament (Ananias and Sapphira in Acts 5:1-10; Elymas the sorcerer in Acts 13:6-11; Herod Agrippa in Acts 12:21-23; and the judgment on Jerusalem in Matthew 23:37-39 and other towns in Matthew 11:21-23). But that's not the emphasis of the New Testament.

B. Eternal Judgment

The New Testament primarily focuses on eternal judgment. It warns that those who rebel against God are lost souls not only in life but forever. John the Baptist warned the Jewish religious leaders of that future judgment, saying, "O generation of vipers, who hath warned you to flee from the wrath to come? . . . he [Christ] will burn up the chaff with unquenchable fire" (Matt. 3:7, 12). John 3:36 says, "He that believeth not the Son shall not see life, but the wrath of God abideth on him." When Paul told Felix about the judgment to come, Felix trembled (Acts 24:25). In Romans 1:18 Paul says, "The wrath of God is revealed from heaven against all ungodliness and unrighteousness of men, who hold the truth in unrighteousness." Paul wrote to the Thessalonians, "The Lord is the avenger of all such, as we also have forewarned you and testified" (1 Thess. 4:6). Hebrews 10 warns of the fury that will devour God's adversaries and says "it is a fearful thing to fall into the hands of the living God" (vv. 27, 31). Hebrews 12:29 says, "Our God is a consuming fire."

James wrote, "He shall have judgment without mercy, that hath shown no mercy" (James 2:13). In 1 Peter 4:17 we read, "The time is come that judgment must begin at the house of God; and if it first begin at us, what shall the end be of them that obey not the gospel of God?" Second Peter 2 speaks about the swift destruction false teachers bring upon themselves and the condemnation that the ungodly will face. Jude uses the destruction of Sodom and Gomorrah as examples of the eternal fire the ungodly will face someday when Christ returns to execute judgment.

The book of Revelation has several warnings about eternal judgment. Revelation 14:10-11 says that unbelievers will "drink of the wine of the wrath of God, which is poured out without mixture into the cup of his indignation; . . . and the smoke of their torment ascendeth up forever and ever; and they have no rest day nor night." In verse 19 we read of an angel that "thrust in his sickle into the earth, and gathered the vine of the earth, and cast it into the great winepress of the wrath of God." Revelation 19:15 says this about Christ's return: "Out of his mouth goeth a sharp sword, that with it he should smite the nations, and he shall rule them with a rod of iron; and he treadeth the winepress of the fierceness and wrath of Almighty God." Those whose names are not found in the book of life at the great white throne judgment will be "cast into the lake of fire. This is the second death" (Rev. 20:14).

Warnings about eternal judgment appear also in the gospels. No one said more about judgment than Jesus did. He spoke of a sin that wouldn't be forgiven (Matt. 12:31) and the danger of losing one's soul forever (Mark 8:36). He spoke of destruction (Luke 21:20-24), outer darkness, and weeping and gnashing of teeth (Matt. 22:13). His words about judgment were intense. So we shouldn't be surprised that at His return He will say to the unsaved, "Depart from me, ye cursed, into everlasting fire, prepared for the devil and his angels" (Matt. 25:41).

A Loving Warning

Some people think Jesus spoke only of love and kindness, but He also spoke about eternal judgment. Why did He speak of both? Because if you love someone, you warn him if he's in danger. It would be unloving not to warn a person about danger. Therefore if Jesus had not said anything about eternal judgment, we could say He was unloving. But He warned of judgment many times. That shows He really cares about people. Christ wasn't apathetic about the eternal destiny of men. He warned of judgment so that people might be drawn to salvation.

Review

I. THE JUDGE (see pp. 197-201)

II. THE TIME OF JUDGMENT (see p. 201)

III. THE PLACE OF JUDGMENT (see pp. 201-3)

IV. THE SUBJECTS OF JUDGMENT (see pp. 207-14)

Lesson

V. THE PROCESS OF JUDGMENT

A. The Separation

Matthew 25:32 says, "Before [Christ] shall be gathered all the nations; and he shall separate them one from another, as a shepherd divideth his sheep from the goats." Christ will separate people into two groups, just as a shepherd separates his sheep from his goats. Even today in the land of Israel you will see mixed herds of sheep and goats all over the hillsides. Frequently shepherds have to divide them at feeding time and whenever they rest. That's because sheep and goats don't feed well or rest well together. Sheep are docile, easily led, and easily scared. Goats are unruly, fearless, and create all kinds of problems for the sheep. So just as a shepherd separates his sheep from his goats, the Lord Jesus Christ will separate believers from unbelievers at His return. The believers will be taken into His kingdom to join the other saints, and the unbelievers will be put out of His kingdom.

Matthew 25:33 adds another detail about the separation process: "[Christ] shall set the sheep on his right hand, but the goats on the left." In ancient Israel the right hand was considered the hand of blessing and honor, the hand of inheritance. The gentle, submissive sheep were preferred over the unruly goats, who represent those who won't receive any blessing. When the patriarch Jacob wanted to bless his grandsons Manasseh and Ephraim, he was careful about whom he put his right hand on, because that person would become the heir (Gen. 48). Joseph, the father of the two boys, wanted Jacob to put his right hand on Manasseh, who was the firstborn. But Jacob put his right hand on Ephraim, because that's who was to receive blessing and inheritance.

B. The Sentencing

1. Of the righteous

What will happen to those Christ places at His right hand? Matthew 25:34 says, "Then shall the King say unto them on his right hand, Come, ye blessed of my Father, inherit the kingdom prepared for you from the foundation of the world." Believers on earth at the end of the Tribulation will be invited to enter Christ's kingdom. They will be able to stay on the earth, for Christ will set up His earthly rule right then and there.

Notice Matthew begins verse 34 by saying, "Then shall the King say unto them." The emphasis of Matthew's gospel is on Jesus as the King. And by the time Matthew writes of Christ's return, He addresses Christ as the

King because He is about to establish His kingdom and begin His reign. In Matthew 24:30 Christ calls Himself the Son of Man, which was a title of humility. But now that He is ready to set up His kingdom, He is called the King. And in Greek, Roman, and Jewish tradition, the favored people of a king or a judge were placed at his right hand.

a) The invitation

On what basis did Christ invite those on His right hand to come into the kingdom? He said, "Come, ye blessed of my Father, inherit the kingdom prepared for you from the foundation of the world; for I was hungry, and ye gave me food; I was thirsty, and ye gave me drink; I was a stranger, and ye took me in; naked, and ye clothed me; I was sick, and ye visited me; I was in prison, and ye came unto me" (Matt. 25:34-36). Some people think those verses teach salvation by works because it seems as if Christ is letting them into the kingdom because of their kindness and social work. However, Matthew 25:34 makes clear the basis for entrance into the kingdom.

(1) It's based on God's blessing

Matthew 25:34 begins, "Come, ye blessed of my Father." The source of those people's salvation was God's blessing. They will enter the kingdom because of God's sovereign grace; God redeemed those people out of His sovereign love. Verse 34 implies the innate reality of salvation and justification.

(2) It's based on an inheritance

The next clue pointing to salvation by grace and not works is the word *inherit* in verse 34. A person inherits something because he is a member of the family. To receive an inheritance from God means you belong to the family of God. That status is achieved by placing your faith in Christ (Titus 3:5; John 1:12). If you are a child of God, you are a joint heir with Christ (Rom. 8:17).

(3) It's based on God's plan

At the end of Matthew 25:34 Jesus says, "Inherit the kingdom *prepared for you* from the foundation of the world" (emphasis added). When God prepared the kingdom, it was for you that He prepared it. You were ordained to be a part of His kingdom (Eph. 1:4-5). And whomever God chose to be in His kingdom will go into it. He won't lose anyone (John 6:39). Notice that the kingdom was prepared "from the foundation of the world." The inhabitants of God's future kingdom were destined to enter His kingdom even before the world was made. They didn't make a place for themselves in the kingdom by being good to people.

So Matthew 25:34 says that the basis of a person's entrance into the kingdom is God's grace, not good works. The good deeds mentioned in Matthew 25:35-36 are merely the fruit that will be manifest in the lives of the redeemed. A passage that expresses the concept in Matthew 25:34 is 1 Peter 1:3-4: "Blessed be the God and Father of our Lord Jesus Christ, who, according to his abundant mercy, hath begotten us again unto a living hope by the resurrection of Jesus Christ from the dead, to an inheritance incorruptible, and undefiled, and that fadeth not away, reserved in heaven for you." Peter was saying that God chose believers by His mercy and has reserved an inheritance in heaven for them.

Christ mentions the good works of those on His right hand to show that judgment can legitimately be based on our deeds because they are a manifestation of what's really inside of us. Redemption results in good works (Eph. 2:8-10). If you're a Christian, it should be obvious by the way you live. Christ won't say, "Come into My kingdom, even though no one but you and I know that you are saved." He will say, "I invite you to come into My kingdom because God has chosen you, and it's obvious you are a chosen one because of the way you lived." The mark of a true believer is righteousness. And in Matthew 25:35-

36, the specific virtue Jesus focuses on is sacrificial love.

How does a believer show sacrificial love? In Matthew 25:35-36 Jesus mentions six ways: by ministering to those who are hungry, thirsty, in need of a place to stay, improperly clothed, sick, and imprisoned. Such people demonstrate they belong to Christ by their good deeds. The kingdom is for those who meet the needs of others. When Christ was on earth, the greatest needs people had were food, drink, housing, clothing, care in times of sickness, and help when they were in prison. Those same needs exist today, along with many others.

b) The inquiry

The response of those invited into Christ's kingdom is amazing. Matthew 25:37-39 says, "Then shall the righteous answer him, saying, Lord, when saw we thee hungry, and fed thee; or thirsty, and give thee drink? When saw we thee a stranger, and took thee in; or naked, and clothed thee? Or when saw we thee sick, or in prison, and came unto thee?" Notice verse 37 begins, "Then shall the *righteous* answer" (emphasis added). It doesn't say, "Then shall the *good doers* answer." Those who are placed at Christ's right hand aren't there because of their own good deeds, but because God imputed righteousness to them.

c) The illustration

How did Christ answer the questions of the righteous? Matthew 25:40 says, "The King shall answer and say unto them, Verily I say unto you, Inasmuch as ye have done it unto one of the least of these my brethren, ye have done it unto me." Who are His brethren? Hebrews 2:11-12 says Christ is not ashamed to call believers His brethren. So Christ was saying in Matthew 25:40, "Whatever you do to meet the need of a fellow Christian, you do to Me." There are other verses confirming that whatever we do to a believer we do to Christ. First Corinthians 6:17 says, "He that is joined unto the Lord is one spirit." Paul says in Galatians 2:20, "I am crucified with Christ: nevertheless I live; yet not I, but Christ liveth in me."

Jesus Himself said, "Whosoever shall receive one such little child in my name receiveth me" (Matt. 18:5). When you strengthen, encourage, or help another believer, you are doing the same thing to Christ. Jesus said, "He that receiveth you receiveth me, and he that receiveth me receiveth him that sent me" (Matt. 10:40).

Proof of True Saving Faith

1. Is shown in your actions

When Christ returns to the world in judgment, some will say, "Lord, Lord, have we not prophesied in thy name? And in thy name have cast out demons? And in thy name done many wonderful works?" (Matt. 7:22). And the Lord will answer, "I never knew you; depart from me, ye that work iniquity" (v. 23). Why didn't Christ ask them into His kingdom? Because good deeds don't qualify a person to enter the kingdom, only the inner reality of salvation by God's grace does. Some people will try to enter the kingdom on the basis of a few good deeds done with a flair. But a true believer manifests the indwelling presence of the living God through continuous acts of love. That's what Jesus calls us to do in John 13:35: "By this shall all men know that ye are my disciples, if ye have love one to another."

The proof of a believer's salvation is in the routine things he does. In 2 Corinthians 13:5 Paul challenges us to examine ourselves to make sure that we're in the faith. Our actions reveal who we really are. Romans 2:6-7 says God "will render to every man according to his deeds: to them who by patient continuance in well-doing seek for glory and honor and immortality, eternal life; but unto them that are contentious, and do not obey the truth, but obey unrighteousness, indignation and wrath." True salvation manifests virtue, godliness, brotherly kindness, and love (2 Pet. 1:5-7).

What did you do last week to meet someone else's needs? When was the last time you put aside a luxury in order to give a needy person something he needed? Have you shared your time, prayers, thoughts, instruction, love, kindness, or substance with anyone recently? Have you recently visited someone who is sick or in prison? Perhaps he has a family who needs your care. A truly redeemed person will manifest his Father's characteristics. That's what Jesus did when He came into the world. When John the Baptist sent a messenger to Jesus to find out if He was the Messiah, Jesus answered, "Go and show John again those things which ye do hear and see: The blind receive their sight, and the lame walk, the lepers are cleansed, and the deaf hear, the dead are raised up, and the poor have the gospel preached to them" (Matt. 11:4-5). He was saying He was indeed the Messiah because He was meeting the needs of hurting people.

It's sad that we live in an utterly indulgent society. We often forget that we ought to be giving of ourselves. Service rendered to another Christian is a mark of true salvation. There will be plenty of opportunities for believers who live through the Tribulation to render service to other believers. Many people will be without food, water, and clothing during the Tribulation. There will be shattered lives and families. There will be sick and imprisoned people. If any believers encounter those difficulties, it will be another believer who comes to their rescue.

Would Christ be able to say to you now, "Come into My kingdom; I know you were chosen before the foundation of the world because I see My Father's love in your life"? The answer lies in what you are doing now for other people.

2. Is shown in your attitude

Notice the humble attitude of the believers in Matthew 25:37-39. They don't know why the Lord is commending them. They won't proudly say, "Yes, Lord, I deserve to enter the kingdom because I was once Philanthropist of the Year." They will say, "God, I did what You wanted me to do, but there was so much more I should have done!"

I'm sure you have felt you could be doing so much more for others. You may recognize that you have been insensitive to the needs of others. We won't always be giving food to the hungry or clothes to the poor because most of us live in a well-to-do society. But there is always a need for encouragement, love, and kindness. A true Christian will seek to meet those needs. John said, "Whosoever hath this world's good, and seeth his brother have need, and shutteth up his compassions from him, how dwelleth the love of God in him?" (1 John 3:17).

In Matthew 25:40 Jesus says, "Inasmuch as ye have done it unto one of the least of these my brethren, ye have done it unto me." Christ identifies Himself with the least of His brethren. Some of us might look at another believer and say, "He's nothing. I'm not going to waste my time on him; I don't want to get involved with his situation." But Christ identifies with that person, and we are to meet his needs. In fact, it's usually the least of Christ's brethren who need the most help.

2. Of the unrighteous

    a) The command

    What will Christ say to those placed at His left hand? Matthew 25:41 says, "Then shall he say also unto them on the left hand, Depart from me, ye cursed, into everlasting fire, prepared for the devil and his angels."

    Hell was prepared for Satan and the fallen angels. The angels, who were once pure and holy, cannot be redeemed, so God made a place of everlasting destruction for them. And with them He will send those who choose to rebel against Him. Notice verse 41 doesn't say hell was made for unbelievers. That's because God created man for fellowship with Himself. But those who reject Him will go away with the rebellious angels into everlasting fire—they will be eternally separated from God.

    In Matthew 25:42-43 Jesus continues, "I was hungry, and ye gave me no food; I was thirsty, and ye gave me no drink; I was a stranger, and ye took me not in; naked, and ye clothed me not; sick, and in prison, and ye visited me not." They never demonstrated the love of God in their lives. They didn't reflect His presence. They never gave of themselves to meet the needs of others.

b) The claim

Those whom Christ condemns will answer Him, saying, "Lord, when saw we thee hungry, or athirst, or a stranger, or naked, or sick, or in prison, and did not minister unto thee?" (v. 44). That's like saying, "Lord, if we had known You were around, we would have met Your need. When did we fail to take care of You?"

c) The confrontation

Matthew 25:45 states Christ's response to those on His left: "Verily I say unto you, Inasmuch as ye did it not to one of the least of these, ye did it not to me." The unregenerate never minister to the saints with love as their motive.

The dialogues in Matthew 25:34-45 tell us two things: people are saved because they are chosen by God, and they are damned because of what they don't do. Those represented by the five unprepared virgins are rejected from the kingdom because they failed to be prepared—not because they were immoral or wretched. They failed to believe in the Lord Jesus Christ. Of the three servants who were entrusted with their master's money (Matt. 25:14-30), which one was rejected? The one who didn't do anything with the talent he was given. Failure to put your faith in the Lord Jesus Christ is all that's needed to condemn you. Without belief in the Lord Jesus Christ, a person lacks the righteousness and love of God.

d) The condemnation

Matthew 25:46 tells us the fate of unbelievers: "These shall go away into everlasting punishment." Zechariah 14 describes some of what will happen at that moment: "The Lord shall be king over all the earth; in that day shall there be one Lord, and his name one. . . . And this shall be the plague with which the Lord will smite all the peoples that have fought against Jerusalem: their flesh shall consume away while they stand upon their feet, and their eyes shall consume away in their holes, and their tongue shall consume away in their mouth" (vv. 9, 12). The people on the Lord's left side will be consumed instantaneously. As Matthew 25:46 says, they will go into everlasting punishment. They will be removed from the earth. And Matthew 25:46 ends by saying, "The righteous [will go] into eternal life."

Some people don't want to believe God will punish unbelievers eternally. But Matthew 25:46 says they will go into everlasting punishment. They will "go into hell, into the fire that never shall be quenched, where their worm dieth not, and the fire is not quenched" (Mark 9:43-44). They will go into an eternity without God. At the end of Christ's thousand-year reign they will return for their final sentencing at the great white throne judgment (Rev. 20:11-15).

Conclusion

Our Lord ended the Olivet discourse with a warning. When is He coming? We don't know the exact moment. We should be ready at all times because irreversible judgment will occur when He comes. At Christ's right hand will be the sheep who received the Savior and were made righteous. Their righteousness will be manifest by their works. At Christ's left hand will be the goats—unbelievers who do not possess or manifest the love of God. The sheep will be invited into the kingdom, and the goats will be removed from the earth and sent into eternal punishment.

There will be only two places in eternity. Every person has to choose where he will be. You will either be in the kingdom or in everlasting fire. And the issue isn't what you do, but what you don't do. Not to receive Christ is to reject Him. And that will ultimately determine your destiny.

Focusing on the Facts

1. What perceptions do many people have of what God was like in the Old and New Testaments? Are the perceptions accurate? Explain (see p. 218).
2. What is the primary nature of the judgment God imparted in the Old Testament? How is it different from the judgment spoken of in the New Testament (see p. 218)?
3. Was Jesus unloving when He spoke about judgment? Explain (see p. 220).
4. What is the first action Christ will take when He returns to judge the world (see p. 220)?
5. What is the significance of being placed by Christ's right hand? by His left hand (see p. 221)?
6. What will Christ say to those at His right hand (Matt. 25:34; see p. 221)?
7. Christ commends those at His right hand for doing the good deeds listed in Matthew 25:35-36. Some people interpret that to mean that salvation is earned by works. How does Matthew 25:34 refute that viewpoint (see pp. 222-23)?
8. Why did Christ mention the good works of those at His right hand (see p. 223)?
9. How did those at Christ's right hand respond to His invitation (Matt. 25:37-39)? What was Christ's answer to their inquiry (Matthew 25:40; see p. 224)?
10. When you strengthen, encourage, or help another _____, you are doing the same thing to _____ (see p. 225).
11. What two things basically prove that a person is saved? Comment on each (see pp. 225-27).
12. What will Christ say to those at His left hand? Why (Matt. 25:41-43; see p. 227)?
13. What claim will be made by the people at Christ's left hand (Matt. 25:44)? How will Christ respond to that claim (Matt. 25:45; see p. 228)?
14. What two things do the dialogues in Matthew 25:34-45 tell us (see p. 228)?
15. What do some people *not* want to believe about the punishment of unbelievers? How do Matthew 25:46 and Mark 9:43-44 refute their wishful thinking (see p. 229)?
16. What is the issue regarding one's eternal destiny? Explain (see p. 229).

Pondering the Principles

1. In Matthew 25:34 Christ affirms that salvation is by grace and not by works. Many psuedo-Christian groups today teach salvation by works. Read John 3:17-18, Romans 3:28, 5:1-2, 10:9-10, and Titus 3:5. Memorize those Scripture references so that you will always be prepared to affirm the teaching of God's Word on the basis for salvation. Another key principle is that even though salvation is by grace, it will be manifest by our works. According to Ephesians 2:8-10, we are saved by grace and "created in Christ Jesus for good works" (v. 10, NASB). God has designed to conform us to the image of Christ, and He is doing it through His power, not our own. That shows the abundance of God's grace to us. Thank Him for His grace, and seek to exalt Him by continually doing good.

2. The reason Christ spoke frequently about future judgment was to call men to salvation. He loves all men and doesn't want to see anyone sentenced to eternal condemnation. Think about the way you have communicated the gospel to non-Christians in the past. Do you usually talk about the benefits of receiving Christ without bringing up the consequences of not receiving Him? It's important to do both. Don't be afraid to warn of future judgment. Let the person know that you are warning him because you love him. The high price of being straightforward may be rewarded by the gain of a new brother or sister in Christ.

Scripture Index

Topical Index